# Helping Children to Cope
# with Change, Stress and Anxiety

*by the same author*

**Helping Children to Build Self-esteem**
**A Photocopiable Activity Book**
2nd Edition
*Deborah M. Plummer*
*Illustrated by Alice Harper*
ISBN 978 1 84310 488 9

**Helping Adolescents and Adults to Build Self-esteem**
**A Photocopiable Resource Book**
*Deborah M. Plummer*
ISBN 978 1 84310 185 7

**Social Skills Games for Children**
*Deborah M. Plummer*
*Foreword by Professor Jannet Wright*
*Illustrated by Jane Serrurier*
ISBN 978 1 84310 617–3

**Anger Management Games for Children**
*Deborah M. Plummer*
*Illustrated by Jane Serrurier*
ISBN 978 1 84310 628 9

**Self-esteem Games for Children**
*Deborah M. Plummer*
*Illustrated by Jane Serrurier*
ISBN 978 1 84310 424 7

**The Adventures of the Little Tin Tortoise**
**A Self-esteem Story with Activities for Teachers, Parents and Carers**
*Deborah M. Plummer*
ISBN 978 1 84310 406 3

**Using Interactive Imagework with Children**
**Walking on the Magic Mountain**
*Deborah M. Plummer*
ISBN 978 1 85302 671 3

# Helping Children to Cope with Change, Stress and Anxiety

A Photocopiable Activities Book

*Deborah M. Plummer*

*Illustrations by Alice Harper*

Jessica Kingsley Publishers
London and Philadelphia

First published in 2010
by Jessica Kingsley Publishers
116 Pentonville Road
London N1 9JB, UK
and
400 Market Street, Suite 400
Philadelphia, PA 19106, USA

*www.jkp.com*

**Library of Congress Cataloging in Publication Data**
A CIP catalog record for this book is available from the Library of Congress


**British Library Cataloguing in Publication Data**
A CIP catalogue record for this book is available from the British Library


ISBN 978 1 84310 960 0


Printed and bound in Great Britain by
MPG Books Limited

## Worries

Last night, I had a sad, sad dream.
And this morning it slipped into my pocket and grew
…into a worry thought.
I carried it around with me all day
…on the walk to school and in the playground and the classroom.
Wherever I went the worry thought came too.

Each time I looked at the thought it seemed to get a bit bigger.
I tried to keep it hidden.
My teacher said, 'You're quiet today –
are you feeling ill?'
I didn't know what to say.
The worry thought grew heavier in my pocket.

My stomach hurt.
I couldn't do my work.
I thought, 'What if my sad dream really happens?
What if it's happening right now and I don't know?'
The worry in my pocket got even heavier.

We lined up for lunch.
Craig tugged my hair and said 'Cheer up!'
I pushed him hard and shouted 'Go away!'
The teacher came and took me from the line.
'Oh no!' she said. 'You mustn't.
This isn't like you at all.'

Mum came to fetch me at home time.
I couldn't tell her what was wrong either
…but she saw the worry spilling out from my pocket
and she scooped it up and took a good look at it.
'What a sad, sad worry,' she said, 'it's grown so big that it needs two of us to carry it.'

We took the worry thought home with us and made some space
…so we could talk with it.
We let it tell its story.
We listened to what it had to say and thanked it for its message.
It started to get smaller.

Then when it was small enough to fold away
Mum and I put the sad, sad worry in my worry box and shut the lid on it tightly
so that tonight…
I'll dream a different dream.

*D.M. Plummer, 2009*

*Dedication*
*For my father, who instilled in me a love of story and encouraged my imagination, and my mother, who taught me not to give up.*

# Contents

ACKNOWLEDGEMENTS                                                          8

PREFACE                                                                   9

## Part One Being There: Interacting Mindfully              13

  1.   Supporting Emotional Well-being                                   15
  2.   Understanding Why we do the Things we do                          21
  3.   Encouraging Imaginative Solutions                                 30

## Part Two Skills for Life                                          39

  4.   Self-awareness                                                    41
  5.   Imagework                                                         50
  6.   Feelings                                                          58

## Part Three Coping with Change                                   67

  7.   Thinking about Change                                            69
  8.   Preparing for Change                                             78
  9.   Making a Change                                                  84

## Part Four Coping with Stress                                    87

  10.  What is Stress?                                                  89
  11.  Changing how we Feel                                             96

## Part Five Coping with Anxiety                                  105

  12.  Thinking, Feeling, Doing                                        107
  13.  What to do with Worries                                         112

## Part Six Moving On                                              127

  14.  Setting Goals and Celebrating                                   129

APPENDIX: CHILDREN'S BOOKS                                              137

INDEX                                                                   139

ACTIVITIES INDEX                                                        141

# Acknowledgements

I would like to acknowledge the influence of Dr Dina Glouberman and my fellow imagework practitioners who encouraged and supported me as I learnt about the power of imagery for my own use, and then as I trained as a practitioner myself. Under Dina's guidance I was able to integrate the use of imagery into my work as a speech and language therapist and as a workshop facilitator. I now also bring elements of this invaluable tool into my work as a lecturer.

There have been many friends in the imagework community who have inspired me with their wisdom and insight. I would particularly like to thank Hermione Eliot and Marsha Lomond who, together with Dina, read draft manuscripts of my first books and encouraged me to seek a publisher. I was lucky enough to be taken on by Jessica Kingsley, who published my first book, *Using Interactive Imagework with Children: Walking on the Magic Mountain* (from which selected material has been revised and updated to form the basis for sections of this book). I would like to thank her for seeing the importance of this work with both children and adults, and for starting me on my writing career.

# Preface

The underlying philosophy of this book is very simple: our interactions with children should always be mindful, based on our understanding of them as unique individuals. It is by listening to what children are telling us and by walking alongside them on their journey of self-discovery and mastery that we can learn most about how they view the world and themselves and therefore how best to support their emotional well-being.

In order to be mindful of children we need to be equally mindful of our own thoughts, feelings and behaviour. This includes recognising how our actions and words can have a profound effect on how our children feel and behave too. I am sure, for example, that every one of us has experienced unwanted stress in our life at some stage and we all have our own ways of dealing with this - sometimes successfully, sometimes not so successfully, perhaps turning to methods that aggravate our stress levels rather than alleviating them. Undoubtedly we are in a better position to help the children in our care if we are also aware of our own strengths, stressors and anxieties and our own ways of coping.

---

Note: Throughout the book I refer to 'your child'. This should also be taken to mean the child or children in your class, group etc.

## Using this book

*Helping Children to Cope with Change, Stress and Anxiety* provides practical activities and strategies for children who are experiencing mild to moderate levels of stress, have difficulty coping with changes in their life or are prone to mild to moderate anxiety.

The book follows a logical sequence of exploration, incorporating elements of a selection of approaches shown to be highly effective in supporting the emotional health and wellbeing of both adults and children. There is particular emphasis on helping children to utilise their imagination to solve problems and gain confidence.

The use of imagery has always formed an important part of my work with both children and adults and you will see that this theme runs throughout the book.

Part One focuses on key elements of a supporting relationship and sets the activities in the context of some of the latest findings concerning brain development and how our thinking affects our behaviour. Part two 'Skills for Life' consists of a range of activities which lay the foundations for the following three sections on change, stress and anxiety. This skills section is an important starting point for all children, regardless of the type of difficulty they are facing.

There is naturally some overlap in the ideas offered in Part Three (Coping with Change), Part Four (Coping with Stress) and Part Five (Coping with Anxiety) since change can itself be a stressor, especially change for which we are ill-prepared, and of course stress and unpredictability can lead to anxiety. It is therefore recommended that you draw appropriate suggestions from all three of these sections to fit the needs of your child.

Finally, Part Six looks at strategies for recognising and celebrating achievements and maintaining progress.

Please remember, if you are concerned about ongoing and persistently high levels of anxiety in your child it is always best to seek support via your child's school or your G.P. This book is not intended as a substitute for the professional help that may be needed when a child is experiencing clinically recognised difficulties such as chronic school phobia, severe social anxiety or childhood depression. It is also not within the scope of this book to look specifically at change resulting from bereavement although many of the activities are appropriate for use with children who are coping with loss.

At any stage in life we do the best we can with the knowledge available to us at the time. Sometimes what seems to work for a friend and their child may not work for you; what works well for your child may not necessarily fit with what is recommended by someone else. The ideas outlined in *Helping Children to Cope with Change, Stress and Anxiety* are therefore offered as suggestions for coping strategies and also as vehicles for a deeper understanding of your child's fledgling attempts at dealing with life. They will also undoubtedly highlight what is already working well for you. This is a vital part of the process. As you select, try out and refine the ideas, remember to acknowledge your skills as a parent or carer – all those strategies that you already use and all the support, love and understanding that you already give to your child.

Before you begin to use the activities in this book, please take some time to ask yourself the following questions. There are no right or wrong answers to these but your responses will give you an indication of a good starting point for supporting your child and will also be a useful way for you to monitor your child's progress.

- What are my best hopes for my child? What would I most like my child to gain from the strategies in this book?

- What are my best hopes for myself? What would I most like to gain from using this book?

- What skills do I have as a parent (or teacher/ carer) to help me to support my child?

- What skills do I have in other areas of my life that I can draw on to help my child in difficult situations?

- On a scale of 1–10 where 1 is hardly any problem at all, how much of a problem do I think my child has with regard to coping with change, stress or anxiety?

- How much do I believe that my child can overcome this?

- How do I cope with change, stress and anxiety in my own life?

- Can I see any similar patterns in how my child copes?

- How much do I feel in control of my own emotions?

- How much do I think my child feels in control of his/her emotions?

- How much do I find my child's anxiety distressing or overwhelming?

- What do I see as my *main* role(s) as a parent? (For example, nurturer, teacher, provider of fun, supporter, rule-maker, protector, encourager, friend, rescuer).

- How do I reflect these roles in the way that I interact with my child? (For example do I tell my child what to do when he is having difficulties? Do I tend to rush in and 'rescue' him when he is anxious?)

- Do I make enough time for myself/ look after myself? What do I need to do to make sure that this is happening?

- What or who has been the biggest influence in my life with regard to being encouraged to fulfil my potential?

*Part One*

# Being There: Interacting Mindfully

# Chapter 1

# Supporting Emotional Well-being

During almost 30 years of training and working as a speech and language therapist, and then as a lecturer in human communication and in health studies, I have attended numerous courses and workshops and stacked up a fair amount of psychology books and personal development books, not all of which have been wise buys! Without a doubt, the strongest influences on the ways in which I have structured my therapy and my teaching have come, not from the 'how to do' manuals that line one side of my study wall, but from the writings and teaching of those inspirational people who understand that 'how to be' is the most important foundation for 'how to do'.

Carl Rogers, the originator of 'person-centred' therapy, was a strong advocate of this approach. He believed that each of us has a natural tendency to strive to achieve our full potential in life, and he proposed that there are certain conditions which will promote this tendency. These became known as the 'core conditions' for a successful therapeutic alliance, but Rogers also made it clear that he felt such conditions were valid for *all* human relationships. He believed that if he maintained a relationship characterised on his part by congruence ('a genuineness and transparency, in which I am my real feelings'), unconditional positive regard ('warm acceptance of and prizing of the other person as a separate individual') and empathy ('a sensitive ability to see his world and himself as he sees them'), then the other person in the relationship would be more self-directing and self-confident and able to cope with life's problems 'more comfortably' (Rogers 1961, pp.37–8).

Most of us recognise the importance of these core conditions in terms of our own relationships, but in our busy lives, and often because of our own early life experiences, it can be easy to forget some of the ways in which we can actually demonstrate these principles to our children. Over the years I have found that there are two very practical strategies which can help children to recognise their own worth and to be more self-directed. The first involves a clear demonstration that we understand, value and respect their feelings. The second involves giving genuine, realistic and specific praise which reflects our belief in each child's unique capabilities.

## Valuing feelings

You will perhaps be familiar with all or some of the following parental concerns.

'I'm tearing my hair out. Kaushika is crying every night and saying that she doesn't want to go to school, but I know that the teachers are really nice and she's got some good friends. I can't understand what's wrong.'

'Terri worries about just about everything! Even the smallest change in her routine upsets her. She makes herself physically sick sometimes with her worrying.'

'Rob has a school concert coming up next term and he's getting stressed about it already. I told him there's no need to worry – he's a great drummer – but he just gets so worked up about everything weeks before it ever happens.'

'Marcus is too young to be getting so many headaches. The doctor says it's stress-related. We've tried everything to get him to relax and think more positively about himself but he seems to think that he's no good at anything.'

'We've been posted to another new place. The children have only just got settled in at school and I'm concerned that another move is going to affect their school work.'

'When his best friend moved away he seemed to go inside himself for months. Now he's mixing with a group of kids who are real troublemakers. I can't get him to see that they're not good friends to have.'

A child's life is inevitably full of changes and times of uncertainty. Some of these changes bring excitement or relief – perhaps the chance to leave unwanted situations behind and move on to make new choices. Others result in sadness, anger or frustration, or a confusing mixture of these emotions. And whilst some children cope remarkably well with change, for others change, even on a relatively small scale, can be a difficult and ultimately stressful experience.

Ideally, children need to be comfortable with a whole range of emotions and able to build emotional resilience and reach an understanding of what causes different feelings. However, for many reasons, this is a difficult developmental task – one which many of us continue to struggle with throughout adulthood. The 'science' of emotions is explored in the next chapter, but there are also many other factors to consider.

The ways in which children experience and express their emotions are partly determined by their developmental level and partly reinforced by the reactions of others, by family and cultural influences, and by past experiences. For example, it may be that our children rarely hear us talking about how we feel. Or we may have inadvertently given them the message that some feelings are not acceptable ('Don't be angry', 'Don't get upset', 'It's nothing to cry about'). This can result in confusion about feelings in general. Is it OK to feel sad when someone dies or moves away but not OK to feel sad when I have lost or broken something? Why do I cry when I feel frustrated or angry? Maybe it's wrong to feel this way? I don't know what I'm feeling!

There are several activities in Part 2: 'Skills for Life' which help children to explore and understand feelings. There is also a very simple three-step technique which can be used as a starting point to help your child to recognise and deal with emotions appropriately. Once the initial intensity of an emotion has subsided, sit quietly with your child and try the following:

**Step 1:** Say what you saw, heard and felt. ('When you shouted at Tom and pushed him away you sounded really angry. Tom fell over and got upset.')

**Step 2:** Make a hypothesis about the feeling. ('It's really tough when you spend ages making something and then someone spoils it. I bet you felt really frustrated.')

**Step 3:** Separate the feeling from the action. ('It's OK to feel frustrated. It's not OK to push your brother like that.')

In this example, the idea of 'frustration' has been offered as an alternative to full-blown anger, giving the child the opportunity to widen his understanding of different levels of emotion. The 'follow-up' to this would be to help him to work out how to do things differently by describing and encouraging a more acceptable way to deal with the feeling, and by helping him to think of a practical solution to the situation that *triggered* the feeling ('Where could you finish making this so that Tom can't reach it?'). If used consistently, this way of showing that you value your child's feelings will have a far-reaching effect on the development of his ability to understand and regulate his emotions.

## Praise

Praise and demonstration of pleasure in a child's abilities, perseverance, sense of fun and so on can be an excellent motivator for continued change and development – but children are usually very good at spotting praise that is not genuine, and will be quick to reject it if it doesn't fit with how they see themselves. Also, unrealistic or unjustified praise could set a child up for experiencing low self-esteem if he tries to do things before he is ready, or if it leads to him developing unrealistically high expectations of what he can achieve. Even when we do offer genuine praise, adults have an unfortunate tendency to add a qualification of some sort! Such qualified praise might go something like:

- 'That's a lovely picture – but you've forgotten his eyes!'
- 'What a great way to share – if only you'd done that this morning you wouldn't have got into a fight!'
- 'Well done for helping out – why can't you always do that without getting grumpy?'
- 'I noticed that you were being really helpful when Sam was upset – you'd usually get cross with him, wouldn't you?'

Similarly, it can be all too easy to offer praise that indicates the lesser achievements of others. An award for the fastest worker or best listener, for example, suggests that there are others who are not so good at this, and also gives little scope for further development. (If I am already the best, I don't need to think about that any more!)

So here are some tried and tested alternatives:

- The most effective approach is to use genuine specific, descriptive praise whenever possible: 'I liked the way you really listened to what Josh had to say about following the rules of the game'; 'I noticed you were being very helpful when Sam got upset, and that really worked because he calmed down straight away!'; 'Your "problem" picture really shows me what it must feel like to be worried all the time. This is what I call thoughtful'; 'You were ace at noticing your worry thoughts and keeping them controlled today'.
- Acknowledge difficulties and empathise with the feelings: 'It looked like it was hard for you to wait your turn. You had lots of great ideas to share! That must have been really frustrating for you!'
- Encourage your child to give descriptive praise to others: 'What did you like about the way that Josh handled that?'
- Encourage your child to use descriptive *self*-praise: 'I caught a really big worry thought just in time today,' or 'I talked to someone new at break time and it was hard, but I felt good afterwards.'
- Expressing your admiration can also enable a child to self-evaluate in a wonderfully productive way: 'That's fantastic! How did you know how to do that?'; 'I had no idea that you knew about the planets/were so artistic/could make a kite. Was that hard to learn?'; 'Tim said that you always remember people's birthdays – that's really impressive! How do you manage to do that?'
- Give non-verbal signals of approval and encouragement. A 'thumbs up', a wink or a smile across a room can be particularly helpful for children who are anxious. You can show that you understand how they feel without rushing in to rescue them.

- Christine Durham, in her book *Chasing Ideas* (Durham 2006), describes a useful way to make praise a fun interaction for older children. She suggests the use of acronyms and abbreviations such as VIP (Very Important Proposition) or IT (Insightful Thinking). This could start as a game in itself – perhaps taking familiar acronyms and familiar sayings and encouraging your child to make up 'secret' messages about behaviour and thoughts. For example, VIP could be 'Very Imaginative Problem-Solver' or ACE could be 'A Cool Example'. Giving your child a 'thumbs up' sign and saying 'ACE' then becomes even more meaningful and fun!

- Encourage your child to reflect on what happens during certain chosen activities and during her daily routines, picking up on the encounters and strategies that are working well and, in particular, any moments of difficulty which have been successfully negotiated.

- Use memory aids if necessary to help you to remember ideas that your child has come up with during some of the activities in this book. Comment on these at a later time to show that you have really thought about what he said.

- A clear demonstration that we value children as unique individuals can be conveyed in the simplest of ways. Telling a child that we enjoy her company, or love talking with her, emphasises the fact that she has a positive 'effect' on us simply by being who she is, and not because of what she does or doesn't say or do.

- Remember the often quoted (but worth repeating!) warning to avoid 'labelling' – even if this is just a private thought. For example, instead of thinking of your child as 'shy' try to be more specific: 'At the moment she is unsure of herself when she first arrives somewhere new. It takes her a while to build the confidence to talk to new people. It might help if we practised some things that she could say.'

- Although some children might find it difficult to recognise their current abilities, achievements and talents, this is always a good starting point before moving on to thinking about targets for learning and future goals for self-development. It is important to continue to acknowledge and celebrate current strengths throughout all the sections of this book. Children generally have very little time in their lives to celebrate where they are at before moving on to the next challenge, the next learning target, the next physical achievement – almost as though we are telling them 'Yes, well done, but that's still not quite good enough'!

In summary, supporting children through times of change and stress involves showing them that we love, value and respect them for who they are, not for what they can do. It involves valuing their emotions, letting them know, for example, that it is ok to feel angry, sad or confused about the changes that are happening in their lives. It involves nurturing their skills by giving realistic, unqualified praise and unconditional hugs! I believe that it also involves celebrating their natural capacity for being creative and imaginative.

# References

Durham, C. (2006) *Chasing Ideas*. London: Jessica Kingsley Publishers.

Rogers, C.R. (1961) *On Becoming a Person: A Therapist's View of Psychotherapy*. London: Constable.

# Suggestions for further reading

Plummer, D. (1999) *Using Interactive Imagework with Children: Walking on the Magic Mountain*. London: Jessica Kingsley Publishers.

Plummer, D. (2007) *Helping Children to Build Self-Esteem* (2nd edition). London: Jessica Kingsley Publishers.

Plummer, D. (2007) *Self-Esteem Games for Children*. London: Jessica Kingsley Publishers.

Rogers, C.R. (1980) *A Way of Being*. Boston, MA: Houghton Mifflin.

## Chapter 2

# Understanding Why we do the Things we do

*Sandra is ten years old. Her father has a new job in another part of the country and has been commuting to and from home at weekends for the last eight months. The family have now made arrangements to move so that they can spend more time together. Sandra's parents have always spoken about the move in very positive terms, and in order not to disrupt their daughter's last year at primary school the move will take place during the summer holidays.*

*Despite her parents' support and positive attitude, Sandra is showing signs of increasing anxiety. Small obstacles now appear to her to be major problems. She is not sleeping well, often waking two or three times in the night having had a 'bad' dream. She appears tired and listless at school and has reverted to some comfort behaviours from her earlier childhood, including wanting to have her bedroom light left on at night. She insists on phoning her father every day while he is at work and is terrified that he will have an accident on his commute home at weekends. She worries that her mother will forget to pick her up from school, that her younger brother will get lost in the shops, that she won't have the right kit for her lessons at her new school, and that she will never make any new friends. Her list of worries is growing each day.*

Sandra may be naturally sensitive to change and prone to anxiety – her physiological system pre-programmed to be in a heightened state of alertness when under stress, constantly on the lookout for anything that could be seen as threatening or dangerous. This hyper-alertness is physically and emotionally exhausting, and anyone in this state will naturally crave to re-establish a sense of normality and control in their lives. Unfortunately, the ways in which we choose to do this, either consciously or unconsciously, can often be detrimental to our well-being.

The rapid and relatively recent growth in the field of neurosciences has provided important insights into the connections between physiological development, early life experiences and what happens when we are under stress. This helps us to understand the best mechanisms for helping children to cope as they grow and change, and to help them to develop strategies that are appropriate and adaptable for all stages of life. In the context of this book, the most important areas to consider are those of emotion regulation, the stress reaction, and the connection between thoughts, feelings and behaviour.

## Emotion regulation

One of the primary developmental tasks in the emotional life of a young child is the establishment of an effective emotion-regulation system: the ability to self-regulate and self-calm so that he or she is not constantly overwhelmed with difficult emotions.

There are two areas of the brain that are particularly important in the development of this self-regulatory capacity: the amygdala and the pre-frontal cortex.

*The amygdala*, a small, almond-shaped area of interconnected structures located on either side of the brain within the temporal lobes, plays a major part in how we experience emotions and is responsible for detecting threat and initiating the stress response (fight, flight or freeze) by sending information to the hypothalamus (which is concerned with regulating various systems within the body, including the release of stress hormones). The amygdala has been shown to be involved in the laying down of immediate and long-lasting emotional memories associated with perceived threat. For example, when a person or object is associated (even by chance) with a traumatic event, the amygdala will produce such a strong neuronal response that a future encounter with that same person or object will trigger the stress response, regardless of whether any actual threat is present (Nunn *et al.* 2008).

The amygdala's primitive and rapid response to threat is, however, mediated by other areas of the brain – for example, the pre-frontal cortex, which deals with feelings and social interactions.

*The pre-frontal cortex*, as its name suggests, constitutes the front part of the frontal lobes. Activation of this area is mood-specific: the left side is associated with positive moods and the right side is associated with negative moods. When the system is working well, impulsive reactions to perceived threat can be inhibited or regulated via the 'thinking' processes carried out at this higher level, thereby preventing us from being overwhelmed, for example, by inappropriate fear and anxiety.

Without a well-developed pre-frontal cortex children will not only have difficulty with self-control and self-regulation, but also with the ability to feel 'connected' to others. This is why very young children are unable to control their impulses to 'lash out', or have a temper tantrum – because the pre-frontal cortex is not yet fully developed.

This area of the brain is most vulnerable to outside influences during its critical period of development in the first four years of life. Such influences include the ability of parents to tune into their child's feelings and provide the comfort and touch which allow the emotion-regulation system to develop and to function effectively. Research shows that where this natural process is inhibited there may be long-term consequences. For example, studies have shown that four-year-olds who have been brought up in highly stressful environments have a measurably smaller pre-frontal cortex compared to four-year-olds who have experienced a nurturing environment. These children show clear signs of lack of social competence, an inability to manage stress and the inability to see things from another child's viewpoint (Gerhardt 2004).

All children, however, experience some stress in their lives without this producing such adverse effects. Moderate amounts of stress are a natural part of growing up, so it is useful for us to understand the normal stress response.

## The stress reaction

'Stress' is a word we are all very familiar with. In everyday language it is generally used to indicate the negative effects of life pressures: 'I feel stressed out'; 'I'm so stressed, I can't think straight'; 'My migraines are getting more frequent because of the stress I'm under.' In fact, of course, a certain amount of stress is useful and necessary. It is one of the factors which motivate us to achieve; it can be a stimulus for action and is an important element for success in many areas of performance, such as music, dance and sport. Moderate or short-term amounts of stress can enhance memory and learning (whereas prolonged stress is known to reduce memory capacity and the ability to learn). Coping successfully with a stressful but potentially enjoyable situation, such as learning to swim or to climb trees, can be a real boost to a child's self-esteem.

Every child will be different in the amount of stress that they can deal with successfully and in how they perceive stressful situations in the first place. For example, what one child sees as exciting and stimulating, another may see as completely terrifying.

Understanding stress therefore involves understanding the unique relationship for each individual between his or her environment and his or her personal abilities and temperament.

## Some common stressors for children

One of the biggest stressors for any child is the loss of (or fear of losing) a secure attachment.

The link between parent and child attachment patterns and a child's later ability to self-regulate has been the focus for much research. Attachment is thought to be the most important source of a child's security, self-esteem, self-control and social skills.

> Through this one incredibly intimate relationship, a baby learns how to identify her own feelings and how to read them in others. If the bond is a healthy one…she will feel loved and accepted and begin to learn the value of affection and empathy. At the same time, this relationship will inevitably provide some dose…of frustration, conflict, and shame, which are necessary to round out her emotional education. (Eliot 1999, pp.305–6)

Another, often misunderstood, area of stress is related to communication disorders. Whilst a lot of children seem to cope with speech or language impairment with remarkable fortitude, there are some who become acutely troubled by feelings of anger rooted in the inherent frustrations of their communication difficulty. Many of these children have difficulty in negotiating with others and in verbally 'standing up' for themselves when they have been unfairly accused or their talents and successes go unrecognised. Children with severe language impairments often do not have the vocabulary to label or describe complex emotions, or the internal language capacity (self-talk) to help themselves to regulate their emotions.

These children, often stressed to breaking point on a daily basis, may feel that they have very little control over their lives and very little control over the turmoil of emotions that threatens to erupt at unpredictable moments. Their frustration may lead to anger directed against themselves or against those who don't understand them, at the 'systems' that don't allow them to communicate effectively, or at those who don't take the time to stop and listen.

Some other common stressors for children include:

- school pressures, including exams and starting or changing schools
- unrealistic pressure for consistently high standards of behaviour and conformity to rules
- bullying, teasing, difficulty in making friends, ending friendships, making new friends, feeling 'different' from peers
- illness or physical disability
- persistent under-stimulation (boredom).

## The stress response and sabre-toothed tigers

There are some normal reactions involved in the 'fight, flight or freeze' response. These are all very useful responses to actual threat or danger, and were particularly helpful for our ancestors when faced with an attack from a sabre-toothed tiger!

- The liver releases some of its store of glucose to fuel the muscles, ready to respond.
- The heart pumps harder to get the blood where it is most needed in preparation for greater muscular effort. This may feel like palpitations and may also result in an increase in blood pressure.
- There is therefore less blood elsewhere, and so the skin often goes pale and the movements of the stomach slow down or stop (the cause of a sudden 'sinking feeling' in the stomach).
- The intestines tend to become less active and the salivary glands dry up.
- Breathing becomes faster because the lungs must take in more oxygen more rapidly and also get rid of carbon dioxide.
- The systems that are involved in fighting infections in the body are less likely to be activated. This is why we are more prone to infectious illnesses after periods of prolonged stress.
- We sweat more profusely to help our bodies to cool down.
- The pupils of the eyes get bigger to let in more light, and so increase sensitivity to incoming stimuli.
- The stress hormones, primarily adrenaline, are secreted to keep this stress reaction going.

If the reaction is completed and the 'danger' is dealt with, then the body can relax again. Unfortunately, we often produce the fight/flight reaction in situations that don't actually need a physical response. These things may happen when children are concerned about a test, a potentially difficult conversation, being in the school play or being late for a school trip. What is even more of a problem is that negative self-talk tends to prolong the stress response. If a child tells himself that he can't cope, then his body will continue to stay ready for action.

## The effects of stress

When stress is excessive or continuous over a long period of time, even at relatively low levels, then we will experience a 'toxic' build-up of stress hormones such as cortisol, which is released by the adrenal glands. Cortisol plays a part in raising blood glucose levels and in breaking down fat and other proteins to provide extra energy for the fight/flight reaction. However, high levels of cortisol can affect our memory capacity and will dampen our immune system. This, coupled with a fall in levels of dopamine and serotonin (feel-good hormones) in the pre-frontal cortex, can cause us to feel 'overwhelmed, fearful, and miserable, colouring our thoughts, feelings, and perceptions with a sense of threat or dread, as if everything we need to do is far too hard' (Sunderland 2006, p.87).

Physical signs of stress can include the following:

- disturbed sleeping pattern
- listlessness
- weepiness
- difficulty in concentration/learning
- unwillingness to go to school/clingy
- a fall in academic performance
- persistent habits, such as throat clearing or nail biting
- change in eating patterns (an increase or decrease)
- headaches/aching muscles
- abdominal pain
- changes in behaviour, e.g. becoming more withdrawn, more aggressive or unpredictable
- increased susceptibility to anxiety.

The effects of continued stress at an early age can have far-reaching effects for our emotional well-being, making it more difficult for us to regulate our emotions in later life. This could result in over-reaction to minor stressors and being physically 'on edge', constantly on the lookout for possible dangers and problems, as illustrated in the case of Sandra at the start of this chapter.

## Thinking, feeling, doing

With increasing maturity, a child's thought processes and the ways in which she appraises situations will also start to play a bigger part in how she interprets and regulates her emotions. When she experiences a state of arousal, such as in anxiety, she will check out what is going on around her in order to find an explanation, and will also draw on past events and 'emotion memories'. Although the links that she makes may be largely subconscious, they can still inform her present reactions. In this way, out-of-control experiences of feeling anxious in the past may, for instance, intensify her current physiological arousal, which in turn confirms her appraisal of the situation and intensifies her experience of the emotion.

Images also play an important role in this process. If I tell myself to increase my heart rate, or to sweat, I'm not likely to notice much response! But if I imagine a frightening experience vividly enough, then my body will respond as if it is actually happening. In fact, 'your imaginings can have as much power over you as your reality, or even more' (Tart 1988, p.59).

The influence of past experiences and the developing capacity to appraise situations as potentially threatening or stressful, combined with fluctuations in biochemical levels and the complex interactions between the pre-frontal cortex and the amygdala, conspire to make emotion regulation a real challenge for all of us. It is hardly surprising that children find this a tricky developmental task. However, there is fortunately much that can be done to help. The brain is remarkable in its capacity to adapt and respond to new influences, particularly during early childhood, and there are many natural childhood activities that help to promote this process.

## Taming troublesome tigers

Coping techniques tend to be situation-specific – what works for one stressor may not work well for another. Strategies for coping with stress and change can be focused on dealing with the problem in some way ('There is no need for me to be in this situation'; 'I can change this situation') or might involve changing the way we think about the problem ('This is quite exciting') or learning to tolerate and accept it ('This is stressful but I can manage my stress levels well'). There are also a number of ways of successfully handling the *effects* of stress. These are briefly outlined below, and examples of specific strategies are given throughout the activities in this book.

### Relaxation

Relaxation techniques can be taught to children in a fun way, to relieve physical tension, to help them to relax emotionally and mentally, and to help them to feel at ease with themselves and with their feelings. Effective relaxation results in decreased metabolism and reduced blood pressure and breathing rate. It also produces the subjective feelings of calmness and emotional stability so this is a really vital skill for children to learn.

It is also important to find an enjoyable relaxation method for yourself. There is no substitute for experience! Your own relaxed breathing and relaxed posture will provide a good model for your child to follow and will, of course, produce long-lasting benefits in your own life. Relaxation is a skill that can be learnt and, as with any skill, regular practice is necessary so that it can become part of daily living.

### Play and active relaxation

Enjoyable physical activity is also a good way to relieve the effects of a build-up of stress chemicals and release feel-good chemicals into the body instead. Walking, cycling, playing sport or just playing outside in the fresh air can all be excellent ways to de-stress. For example, gentle rough-and-tumble play and laughter are known to have anti-stress effects, activating the brain's emotion-regulating centres and causing the release of the brain's natural opioids, which induce feelings of pleasure and well-being (Sunderland 2006).

## Positive touch

Levels of hormones such as oxytocin (the hormone known to aid the 'bonding' process after childbirth) and serotonin (the 'feel-good' hormone that helps us to relax) also vary enormously, according to how much positive physical contact children experience. The release of oxytocin triggered by positive touch such as being cuddled by a parent, or given a massage, contributes to feelings of safety and comfort and is associated with the regulation of cortisol. Incorporating a regular period of massage into a child's daily routine can help to increase concentration levels, decrease levels of agitation and aggression and help children to learn skills of empathy and tolerance.

## Breath control

It's very easy to take our breathing for granted because it's an automatic activity and most people don't think about it on a conscious level. If you watch a baby or young child asleep you will see the ideal breathing pattern – slow, deep and regular. The stomach will be rising and falling easily and smoothly. However, breathing patterns can change, sometimes over long periods of time. These changes might be brought about by health problems, or occur in reaction to prolonged stress, or as a result of suppressed emotions ('Big children don't cry'). As well as these long-term changes in breathing, temporary changes will also occur at times of stress and as a reflection of different emotions. For example, anxiety often results in shallow, rapid breathing. Calm breathing will help children to see that they can have some control over their body when they are feeling nervous or stressed, and can help in dealing with potentially overwhelming emotions such as anger or fear.

## Imagery

The imagination is a valuable inner resource which can be used to foster creative thinking, healthy self-esteem and the ability to interact successfully with others. Creative imagery can provide a rich learning experience that goes beyond the teaching of skills as a way of coping 'after the event' and opens up the possibility of a much deeper learning instead – the type of learning that leads to socially intelligent interactions and promotes feelings of personal fulfilment and self-respect.

There have been many studies highlighting the positive benefits of using images to effect changes in the body. Dr Karen Olness, Professor of Paediatrics, Family Medicine, and International Health at Case Western Reserve University, Ohio, has demonstrated how image messages can have an effect in the treatment of migraines. She has shown that children who regularly practise a relaxation imagery exercise have far fewer migraines than children taking conventional medicine for the same purpose. She has also used such imagery as an adjunct to conventional therapy for children who stammer. Olness, who uses biofeedback systems to show children how 'thinking' can affect their body, feels that it would benefit every child, beginning at age six or seven, to have an opportunity to be connected to a biofeedback system in order to experience the realisation of 'Change my thinking, and my body changes' (Olness 1993).

Imaginative and creative play is also known to reduce levels of stress chemicals, enabling children to deal more successfully with stressful situations.

By encouraging children to listen to their thoughts and feelings and to note how their imagination can affect their bodies, we are teaching them to value themselves, and this will undoubtedly affect the way they interact with others, and the way they deal with situations in the future. Use of the imagination is an important element of the activities introduced throughout this book.

The next chapter offers a brief explanation of imagework and explores the idea of helping children to utilise their natural abilities to create positive future choices.

## References

Eliot, L. (1999) *What's Going on in There? How the Brain and Mind Develop in the First Five Years of Life.* New York: Bantam.

Gerhardt, S. (2004) *Why Love Matters. How Affection Shapes a Baby's Brain.* London and New York: Routledge.

Olness, K. (1993) 'Self-regulation and Conditioning.' In B. Moyers (ed.) *Healing and the Mind.* London: Aquarian/Thorsons.

Sunderland, M. (2006) *The Science of Parenting.* London: Dorling Kindersley.

Tart, C. (1988) *Waking Up. Overcoming the Obstacles to Human Potential.* Shaftesbury: Element.

## Suggestions for further reading

Goleman, D. (1996) *Emotional Intelligence. Why it Can Matter More than IQ.* London: Bloomsbury.

Madders, J. (1981) *Stress and Relaxation* (3rd edition). London: Macdonald and Co.

Nunn, K. (2008) Who's Who of the Brain. London. Jessica Kingsley Publishers.

Sapolsky, R.M. (2004) *Why Zebras Don't Get Ulcers* (3rd edition). New York: Henry Holt and Company.

*Chapter 3*

# Encouraging Imaginative Solutions

## What are images?

Imagine yourself peeling and then chopping an onion with a sharp kitchen knife. Do you see the onion? Can you smell it? Can you imagine the texture of the skin and the different layers as you start to chop it? Do you imagine your eyes watering? Can you hear the sound of chopping?

What images do you have when you think of the following?

- a waterfall cascading down a mountainside
- a freshly mown lawn
- stroking a cat
- waiting at a busy railway station
- attending an important interview.

Which was your strongest sense – touch, sight, sound, smell? Were you aware of any emotions associated with the images? Perhaps you experienced a mixture of all these things, but to varying degrees. Whatever you saw, felt, heard or smelled was, of course, in your imagination and the strength of each of your images will have been a result, in part, of your previous experiences and memories. For example, someone whose main experiences of railway stations are of saying goodbye to loved ones is likely to have very different feelings or 'energy' connected with their images, compared to someone who travels a great deal for pleasure and has a sense of excitement associated with train journeys. A freshly mown lawn could conjure up memories of pleasant summers – or it could perhaps engender feelings of discomfort associated with allergies.

In this way, even if two people visualise the same idea, they will experience it very differently; each person's imagery is unique to them.

The perception and internalisation of a multitude of different visual, auditory, olfactory and kinaesthetic, or 'felt', images is a natural part of our lives. Images are our earliest means of making sense of the world. They form the basis of our knowledge about ourselves and others and about our environment, long before we are able to communicate through words.

Throughout life we build up a memory bank of images; one which reflects our uniquely personal interpretations of our environment and of our experiences and interactions. Whilst many of these may be recalled fairly easily, there are countless others which pass into our unconscious minds, stored away in the 'vaults' and yet still capable of informing our daily lives. Sometimes they influence us to such an extent that we may feel as though we have little choice about our feelings, attitudes or actions.

For example, have you ever felt uncomfortable with someone for no obvious reason? It may be that they 'remind' you of an unpleasant encounter with someone else, even though you are not consciously aware of this connection. Similarly, you may have experienced the effects of the unconscious when you have suddenly felt angry or sad about something and wondered 'Where did that come from?' or 'It's not like me to get upset over that!' Of course, pleasant feelings can also be evoked by unconscious associations – a sound, a smell, or perhaps the sight of a certain object may trigger a feeling of happiness, contentment, and so on, because of its link with past events.

There will also be many images and happenings in life that enter our unconscious subliminally. We will not have taken conscious note of them in the first place, yet they are stored as memories and can be made available to the conscious mind – for example, in moments of 'insight' or after a period of deep thought.

We have all experienced these 'creative ideas', though we may not have been aware of using any specific technique to access them. For example, when a problem seems unsolvable, switching conscious attention away from it and involving yourself in some other activity (going for a walk perhaps) can often result in a solution suddenly 'coming to mind'. Perhaps you have had the experience of solving a problem during dreaming or while meditating. You may have found that you have had sudden flashes of inspiration when you are practising relaxation techniques. The more deeply relaxed you are in both mind and body, the more likely this is to happen.

## Imagework

Constructive use of the imaginative process is a vital part of a child's development, and yet, as we grow into adulthood, the majority of us start to lose touch with this ability. We relegate the imagination to times of daydreaming and discourage our children with such comments as 'Don't be silly, it's only your imagination.' It seems that for most of us the imagination eventually becomes synonymous with things that are 'different' from, and perhaps compensate for, the realities of life, but which are unlikely ever to come true for us. This belief is reflected in some of the following definitions of imagination, given to me by a group of teenagers:

'Pictures and stories and dreams that you form in your head.' *Chloe, 16.*

'Something that thinks things up the way you want them, not the way they are.' *Ruppa, 16.*

'The part of you that can make up anything you want.' *Stuart, 17.*

'Where your best things happen to you.' *Sharon, 16.*

'A place where bad things don't happen.' *Katie, 16.*

'A place inside you where all your dreams are kept.' *Frances, 15.*

It is surely time to rectify this situation, since the tools *are* available to help youngsters to realise some of their 'internal dreams'. I believe that imagework can play an important part in this realisation. By using the power of the imagination in a positive way, children can begin to alter their personal futures and promote their own development towards confidence and well-being.

The term 'imagework' was created by Dr Dina Glouberman, who leads imagework training courses internationally. Imagework is interactive (involving dialogue with the images, either internally or through a facilitator) and organic, allowing for its creative application in many different fields of personal and professional development. Interacting with our images can lead us to find out things about ourselves and the way we see the world in more depth than we are consciously aware of.

The idea of interacting with personal images is not new, of course. The process is centuries old and played an important part in the healing traditions of many ancient cultures. In the nineteenth century Carl Jung developed the idea of 'active imagination' and encouraged his patients to use it as a self-help tool. Active imagination starts from the premise that the unconscious has its own wisdom and so, although a person is participating fully in the process, she allows her imagination to flow where it wants and then works with whatever images arise.

James Hillman advises us to remember that images do not require interpretation (see, for example, 'Imaginal Practice' (Hillman 1990)). He suggests that the image itself is more important, more inclusive and more complex than what we have to say about it. In other words, images demand respect, not analysis! It is important to remember this when helping children to use their imagination. We can encourage them to talk about their images and to talk *with* their images, but we should resist any temptation to offer our own interpretations as to what they might mean. Images are generally very personal to the individual. They should be seen in the context of where, when and how they were created, and in the light of each child's way of viewing the world.

This element of uniqueness in images also means that both stored and newly created images come in many forms. Although many people find that they can 'see' things in their imagination, this is by no means the case for everyone. Some people may get a 'sense' of an image, but not a clear picture. They may be more aware of the sound or smell or feeling associated with it. None of these experiences is 'better' than another, and no matter how we experience images, it is possible to train ourselves to become more aware of them and to create new ones for ourselves.

Below is a brief imagework exercise for you to try. You may need to read through this a couple of times before starting, or ask someone else to read the instructions to you. Have a large sheet of paper and some coloured pencils near by.

> Sit quietly for a few minutes and let yourself relax as fully as possible… Gradually close your eyes… Allow your imagination to come up with an image for the question 'Where am I in my life right now?' This might be an image of an animal, a plant or an object. Just allow whatever comes to mind. Now, in your mind, examine the image very closely… When you are ready open your eyes and sketch the image on paper… When you have finished, sit quietly again with your eyes closed.
>
> Breathe deeply and relax. Allow an image to emerge for the question 'What is my next step?' Explore whatever image comes to you… When you are ready, open your eyes and draw the image.
>
> Repeat this process for the following two questions: 'What is getting in my way/holding me back?' and 'What quality do I need to develop in order to get me through this block?'
>
> When you have drawn the fourth picture, take some time to think about how these images relate to your questions. You might find it helpful to talk to someone about what you have drawn in order to clarify what it all represents. Remember, though, that no one else can interpret your images for you. They are very personal and will trigger your own unique associations. Only you know what significance they have.

## Using imagework to set goals

Imagework can be useful as an aid to setting goals – an important but often undervalued skill. A child who sets herself goals and is ready and able to evaluate her own progress on an ongoing basis will find that she has a clearer sense of direction and purpose and can accomplish more in a short period. A sense of control leads to higher self-esteem, which is more likely to result in higher achievements.

However, many children don't set themselves goals because they have had past experience of failure, or because they have heard too often that they will not be able to achieve them. The idea that this is now true ('I never manage to do what I really want') becomes their own self-limiting belief.

Imagework can provide a child with an opportunity to project himself forward in time in his imagination and see a positive outcome for a desired goal, experiencing it in his conscious mind and, in effect, creating a memory of the event as if it had already happened.

This forward projection will also give a child the opportunity to recognise where he is at the moment – how far along the road he has already come – and to discover some of the things that he will need to know to achieve his goal. Perhaps other people will need to be involved, and he can visualise how this might come about. He can also explore some of the things that might hold him back, things that he will have to overcome to achieve his goal.

For example, inventing a new 'role' for himself in his imagination, where he sees himself achieving a goal, being confident or being assertive, will enable him to experience a new way of acting and reacting and allow him the chance to realise a new set of potentials. Such imagery makes use of the 'as if frame', an idea derived from the work of Richard Bandler and John Grinder (1989). The 'as if frame' enables the gathering of information that is usually unavailable. It requires the suspending of judgement and reality in order to act 'as if' you had already achieved some desired outcome. This concept is already widely used by Olympic athletes, who often have a personal imagery coach. These athletes are taught that by *imagining* themselves performing at their maximum level, they can improve their actual performance.

## Imagework and change

Imagework can also be used to help children to minimise the possible difficulties involved in change by giving them an opportunity to 'research' the risk in their imagination. This will enable them to get a sense of what the possible outcome and benefits might be when they have completed the intended change.

Through imagework children can face some of their fears and put them more into perspective, thereby allowing the possibility of creative solutions to any obstacles. In order to overcome unwanted feelings of anxiety they can be helped to 'reframe' an impending change ('What if you had already done this? See yourself making the change. What is happening?'). They can be encouraged to look at their dilemmas from different perspectives, explore what it would be like to act in a different way, or reach a compromise in order to make the change more manageable for themselves.

As facilitators in this process it is important for us to recognise that obstacles to change are a form of self-protection and should always be respected as such. This means that we need to allow children the opportunity to work through any resistances in their own time and not because we think it would be 'good for them'. Obstacles are usually the best indicators of the most appropriate solution, and this is often clearly illustrated in imagework. The following is an example of how this might work.

*Sarah had great difficulty in making friends at her new school. Her attempts at joining in the games played by other children were awkward and frequently misconstrued as interference. She was seen as 'different' and experienced people's reactions to her as rejection. Before long she gave up attempting to join in and would simply watch from the sidelines or involve herself in elaborate but solitary make-believe. In imagework Sarah saw herself behind a huge brick wall. She could hear the children on the other side and she could sometimes see them through a little peep-hole, but they could no longer see her. The brick wall felt strong and protective, shielding her from harm. Removing this wall would undoubtedly have been devastating for her, but the protection was also compounding her isolation. Sarah came up with some creative alternatives. She found that, in fact, at one end the wall was not attached to anything and would therefore allow her to make short forays to the other side, retaining the possibility of a quick return if needed. She could invite one other child to join her behind the wall to take part in a game of Sarah's own choosing, and then accompany this child back to the main group. If the wall was to be taken down one brick at a time, she felt that she would need someone to help her and it would have to be very gradual, so as to prevent it from collapsing completely and causing damage to herself.*

I could imagine Sarah eventually stepping over a much diminished wall, some time in the not too distant future!

Once you are familiar with the use of imagery, you will find that the strategies become second nature, and you will soon be encouraging children to 'image' problems, decisions, dilemmas and feelings. You can also *offer* images if it seems appropriate – 'When you were really angry with Michael just now, I got this image of a tiger that had been hurt. Is that how you felt?'; 'This problem seems like a huge lump of rock to me – we just can't seem to shift it. What could we do about this rock?' Children who are used to this way of exploring images are often more than willing to put you right and to suggest their own images if they think you haven't quite grasped the essence of what they are feeling: 'No, it's more like a big, swampy puddle…!' Simply talking about images in this way often enables a child to see solutions, or precipitates a shift in perception where none seemed possible before.

By valuing the wisdom of the imagination we can encourage children to use their natural image-making capacity to cope with potentially stressful situations, to help them to solve problems and achieve their goals, to increase their confidence and to help them to overcome the challenges they face in life – in short, to develop themselves. As Einstein said, 'Your imagination is your preview of life's coming attractions.'

## Guidelines for imagework

There are a few guidelines that will help you and your child to enjoy imagework as fully as possible.

### Introducing the idea of imagework

Talk about imagework with your child before you start to use the exercises. There are some activities in Chapter 5 of this book to help you get going. At a very basic level this might be simply a case of talking about having 'thoughts and pictures in your head that help you to work things out'. You might include the idea that imagework helps us to be inventive in how we solve problems, how it can help us to feel more confident, and how it gives us the chance to try things out in our minds before we actually do them.

### Making it 'special'

Make imagework sessions special by allotting a regular time to them, perhaps once a week. As with many important and useful skills in our lives, it is often when we need imagework most that we tell ourselves we don't have the time! Ensuring a regular imagework 'space' in the daily rush of life will have long-term benefits which far outweigh the initial time given.

### Allowing images to emerge

Children are usually very quick to perceive images, but if your child indicates that she is having difficulty you can help her by using any or all of the following suggestions:

- 'There is plenty of time. As you watch just let the image (or pictures) come to you.'
- 'Don't worry if it's a little bit fuzzy to start with. It will fill out gradually as you go along.'
- 'Imagine that you are looking at a story book and you can see the pictures that go with the story you are hearing.'
- 'Don't worry if you can't see the images clearly. Maybe you can get a feeling about them.'

## *Reading the imagework instructions aloud*

Where there is a series of dots in the imagework exercises in this book, this indicates that you need to give plenty of time to let your child explore an image. Keep your voice as calm as possible, both for the imagework sections and, of course, when you are doing the relaxation exercises. Above all, have fun!

The next section, Skills for Life, explores strategies for building the foundation skills needed for coping with change, stress and anxiety. These skills involve supporting your child in developing his self-awareness, in understanding the use of imagery and in understanding his emotions.

# References

Grinder, H. and Bandler, R. (1989) *The Structure of Magic 1: A Book about Language and Therapy.* Palo Alto, CA: Science and Behavior Books, Inc.

Hillman, J. (1990) 'Imaginal Practice.' In T. Moore (ed.) *The Essential James Hillman: A Blue Fire.* London: Routledge.

# Suggestions for further reading

Glouberman, D. (2003) *Life Choices, Life Changes: Develop Your Personal Vision with Imagework* (revised edition). London: Hodder and Stoughton. (First published by Unwin Hyman 1989).

Johnson, R. (1989) *Inner Work: Using Dreams and Active Imagination for Personal Growth.* New York: HarperSanFrancisco.

Tyrrell, J. (2001) *The Power of Fantasy in Early Learning.* London and New York: Routledge.

*Part Two*

# Skills for Life

## Chapter 4

# Self-awareness

By doing the activities in this section you
will be helping your child to:

- think about lots of different aspects
  of himself, not just how he is
  dealing with any difficulties he may be facing

- put specific changes into a broader context

- see himself as an active participant in change

- identify his strengths

- think about what he would like to achieve.

## 1. Self-portraits (p.45)

Use the 'magic mirror' for your child to draw a self-portrait. This
encourages physical self-awareness, but can also be used to help
your child to identify some of the personal skills that he is building
as he tries out the activities in this book. Portraits can be drawn at
different stages. For example, when he has successfully coped with
an important change, he could draw himself with a different expression, wearing different clothes, or perhaps holding something
or doing something that shows what he has achieved.

Display the portraits on a wall or keep them in a journal or a
special folder which can be used for all the activity sheets and
drawings that you do together.

*Talk about:*

- What do you most like about being you?

- What would you most like to change?

- How are your eyes different to your friend's/brother's/sister's eyes? What
  makes your eyes special?

- How are you different from the way you were a year ago? What has
  changed the most?

## 2. Is this how you see me?

Ask your child to collect six descriptions of himself that he likes (words or phrases used by other people to describe him). Encourage a selection of physical descriptions (tall, short, blue eyes, curly hair, etc.) and descriptions of personality/ temperament (happy, thoughtful, etc.).

*Talk about:*

- How accurate does your child think these perceptions are?
- If his grandmother/teacher/uncle says he is artistic or confident, how much would he agree with this?
- Sometimes we think that someone feels a certain way, but this may not be how she actually sees herself. For example, a child might appear to others to be very clever, but she might think that she is not clever compared to an older brother or sister. Is one observation 'more right' than another, or just a different way of looking at things?

## 3. I am me (p.46)

Ask your child to draw a picture or write about himself on the activity sheet.

Writing (or drawing) a self-characterisation can help children to become more self-aware and can reveal important themes about how they see themselves, what worries them, what they enjoy doing, etc. Some children need prompts, such as: 'What would your best friend say about the way that you _____?' but don't be tempted to filter ideas at this stage. Accept whatever your child tells you without judgement, even if you disagree with his perceptions. This activity can be repeated later on, when you feel that your child has begun to make some noticeable changes in the way that he thinks and behaves in difficult situations.

## 4. Everyone is different

Think about two different people in the family, or two of your child's friends. Make a list together of all the ways in which these two people are different from each other.

*Talk about:*

- What would life be like if each of us were exactly the same?
- Imagine what your family would be like. What about your class, or your street or town, or the world?!

- What would be one good thing about everyone being the same? Think about 'sameness' in such things as looks, actions, likes and dislikes.
- What would not be good about all being the same? Why would that be difficult? And then what would happen?'

## 5. Something in common? (p.47)

Invite your child to draw a picture of someone she knows well and who she thinks is similar to her in some way.

*Talk about:*

- Sometimes you can find ways that people are similar. For example, people can be alike in the way that they look, how they behave, where they live, what they like to do or to eat, and what they don't like.
- Think of someone in your class or group who is like you in some way. What is his or her name? How is this person like you?
- Do you know someone who is like you in lots of ways? What is his or her name? How is he or she like you?
- What is good about knowing people who have the same or similar interests as you?
- We are all unique, but we can have things in common with others as well.
- It is natural to want to feel accepted and liked. Feeling part of a group and being accepted and appreciated by a group gives us a sense of belonging and helps us to feel good about ourselves. But sometimes we can find ourselves behaving in ways that don't feel right, just so we can be part of a group because we think it's 'cool' or it's exciting. There may be times when this is OK and also times when it's not OK, when trying to fit in leads to feeling awkward or unhappy. Then we have to be strong and make a different choice.
- Do you think anyone else has the same or similar worries as you have?

## 6. My display cabinet (p.48)

Ask your child to draw pictures in the display cabinet to show some things that are important to her (e.g. an important person, a special fact, my favourite food, my best toy/game, an important day, the thing I hate most).

*Talk about:*

- There are many different types of things that can have a special meaning for us.
- It's important to celebrate our own and other people's achievements.

- Significant events may not always be pleasant.

## 7. My record of achievements

Make brightly coloured stars, flags or badges to help your child to recognise and celebrate her achievements. These can be much more powerful than stickers because they can be uniquely personalised (see also notes on praise on p.17).

## 8. Things I would like to achieve (p.49)

Make a list or draw three things that your child would like to achieve. These might be achievements related to change, stress or anxiety, general achievements, or a mixture of both. Sometimes children end up with a mixture of realistic aims and some that are not achievable in the short term. These can be discussed briefly so that your child can choose which aims to focus on. Once again, do not reject any of your child's aims – even amazing, possibly unrealistic, dreams for the future can be acknowledged as an exciting thought! There are later activities related to setting goals and being specific in deciding on the steps that need to be taken (see activities in Part Three).

## 9. Story treasures (1)

Read a story together about differences and similarities or self-discovery. For the younger age group (around 5–7 years) I have used *Something Else* by Kathryn Cave and Chris Riddell – a beautiful story about Something Else, who tries to be like others but just isn't!

*Nothing* by Mick Inkpen is about a toy's search to 'discover who he really is'.

*Bill's New Frock* by Anne Fine explores the differences between girls and boys. A funny and thought-provoking book for older children, around 7–11 years, this can lead to discussions about expectations and children's views on how adults treat girls and boys.

## 10. Tell me my story

Youngsters love to hear stories about themselves and it is really worth spending time retelling these. Take turns to tell the story of important life events, such as 'The day I started school', 'When I lost my front teeth', or 'When we moved house'.

Providing a theme which you know is familiar is a good way to help your child to explore similarities and differences in how you both cope with situations.

## The Magic Mirror

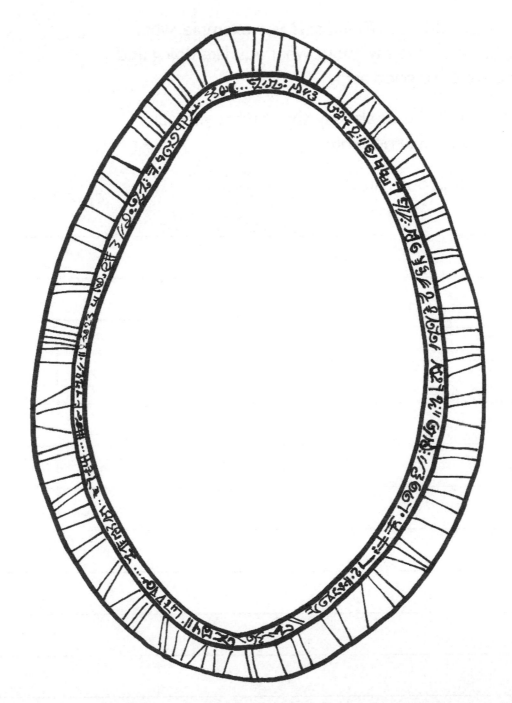

## Look in the mirror and draw a picture of yourself

## I am me

Imagine that you are your best friend talking about you.

What would your friend say? For example, what might he or she say about what you like doing and what you are good at?

What might he or she say about what you *don't* like doing and about what worries you?

Begin with your name:

_____ is _____

_____

_____

_____

_____

_____

_____

_____

_____

_____

## Something in common

**Draw a picture of someone you know well**

## My display cabinet

Imagine that you have a special place where you can put important things on show for everyone to see.

Think of some important things about you that you would want to put on display.

## Draw or write about the things that you would like to achieve

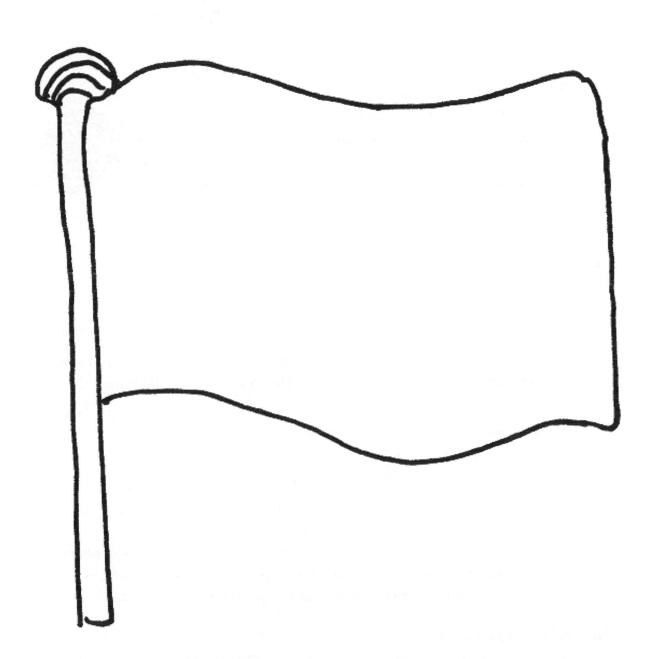

## Chapter 5

# Imagework

By doing the activities in this section you will be helping your child to:

- find out how she can use her imagination in a positive way
- understand that what we think affects how we feel
- understand how different feelings might lead to different ways of behaving.

## 1. What are images? (p.55)

Ask your child to draw something that comes from her imagination.

*Talk about:*

- Have you ever made up a story in your head? Imagined that you saw something that wasn't really there? Heard a noise and imagined that it was something scary?
- Have you ever remembered the taste or feel of something that wasn't actually in front of you?
- Do you ever imagine that you are somewhere else or doing something different?
- These are all images and they come from your imagination.
- We all have the power of imagination, and we can all use our imagination to help ourselves to sort out problems, feel good, cope with troubles when they come along, and do the things that we want to do.

## 2. Think of a chocolate cake

(My niece is one of those rare children who dislikes the taste of chocolate! If your child doesn't like or is allergic to chocolate, then you can substitute any other food here that you know she would love to eat!)

Read the imagery exercise 'Think of a chocolate cake' slowly, with plenty of pauses for your child to really explore the images. Reassure her that there is no right or wrong answer. If she seems unable to 'see' images, that's OK. (In my experience, however, children are usually very quick to produce visual images.)

Encourage your child to tell you about the images. This keeps a feeling of connection between you both and will help you to pace the exercise. For example, when you say 'What does it [the cake] look like?' give your child plenty of time to describe the sort of chocolate cake she is imagining. Show that you are imagining the same image by repeating back what you have heard her say, or by making some appropriate sound ('Mmmmmm!').

## Think of a chocolate cake

Let's check out what your imagination is like today.

Sit comfortably and close your eyes. Imagine that you are in the kitchen. Imagine that it is your birthday and someone has made you a huge chocolate cake. It is in the fridge. You are allowed to go and get it.

Imagine yourself opening the fridge door. You see the cake on a big plate. What does it look like?… You take it out of the fridge. What does the plate feel like? How do you carry the cake? What can you smell?

You put the plate with the cake on it onto a table. Someone comes and cuts a big slice for you. What does this person say while they are cutting the cake? What happens to the cake as this person starts to cut it?

You reach out to take the piece of cake. What does it feel like when you touch it? Then you take a big bite. What can you taste? Can you smell anything? What do you imagine yourself saying? Now let the images fade and, when you're ready, open your eyes.

See how good you are at imagining things!

*Talk about:*

- There are lots of different types of images. Some are like pictures, some are sounds (like imagining a conversation or a tune in your head), some are feeling or sensation images (like imagining the feel of velvet or mud, or imagining what it's like for your friend to feel sad).

- Sometimes we can experience a feeling like sadness or anger or being happy just by imagining something. Can you think of a time when this has happened to you?

## 3. Talking cats (p.56)

Read the activity sheet together.

*Talk about:*

- If we do something regularly, we stop thinking about it too much after a while and just do it, but we can still imagine it or recall the pictures from our mind when we want to. In the same way, when something new is about to happen we can imagine what it might be like.

- We can also imagine things that may never happen at all. Sometimes this is useful, and sometimes we may make up things that worry us and we begin to believe that they are true.

## 4. If I were an animal

This exercise uses one of the basic formats of imagework: becoming the image in order to find out more about it.

Read the following instructions aloud slowly to give your child time to think about what is happening in his imagination. As for Activity 2 in this chapter, ask for feedback as you go along. When you have finished, encourage your child to draw the animal that he chose.

### If I were an animal

Close your eyes and take three deep breaths, letting the air out slowly as you breathe out…

When you are ready, I'd like you to imagine that you could be any animal you wanted. What animal would you be?…

Now imagine that you **are** this animal… Step into being the animal and really feel what that is like… Do you make a sound? What sounds do you make?… Do you move?… If so, how do you move?… Where do you live?… What do you like doing?… What do you not like doing?… What is the best thing about being you?… What is the worst thing?… What would you most like to be able to do?… What do you most wish for?…

Now step out of being this animal and back to being you. Give yourself a shake all over. Shake your legs…shake your arms…and your hands… When you are ready, open your eyes.

*Talk about:*

- All the different characteristics of the chosen animal.

- Are there ways in which you are already like this animal? If not, what animal do you see yourself as right now? How are the two animals different?
- Which animal is your brother/sister/friend like? Why do you think that?

## 5. Feeling good about being me (p.57)

Read the activity sheet together, then read the following exercise to your child and see if you can both use your imagination to help you to stretch further than you thought you could.

Imagine that you are a cat. When cats have been sitting still for a while, or when they have been asleep, they like to stretch out from their noses to their tails. See if you can stretch like a cat. Kneel down with your hands on the floor in front of you. Gradually begin to stretch your arms forward, walking your hands along the floor, feel your body getting longer and longer… Now bring your hands back to just in front of you and start to stretch out your legs behind you instead. First one and then the other…

Now lie on your back on the floor and stretch out your arms, spread your fingers as wide as they'll go… Stretch out your legs and point your toes toward the other side of the room… Now let everything relax again… Gently roll over onto your side and then very slowly sit up.

Now curl yourself up into a ball, and when I say 'go' uncurl and stand up, reach up towards the ceiling as high as you can, really stretching your fingers upwards and standing on tiptoes. 'Go'.

Well done! Now relax again and slowly curl up in a ball. I want to show you how clever your mind is.

Instead of really stretching this time, I want you to **imagine** that you are uncurling and reaching for the ceiling. You can reach right up, way above your head. You can touch the ceiling. You're so good at stretching you can go much further than you thought was possible. In your imagination feel what it's like to stretch that far. See yourself doing it… Good.

Now I want you to **really** uncurl and stretch up and see how far you go… When you imagined doing this you told your body that it could stretch much further than the first time you did it…and it worked!

Now relax, and then give yourself a little shake all over. Shake your arms and your hands. Shake your legs and your feet, shake your shoulders, shake your body…

## 6. Story treasures (2)

Read a story together that explores the imagination. The following books are recommended for children of around 7–11 years of age.

- *And to Think That I Saw It on Mulberry Street* by Dr Seuss is a little boy's tale of his journey from school to home. He wants to tell his dad what he has seen but he thinks that the horse and wagon that he spotted is far too boring to report. By the time he gets home this simple sight has grown into the most amazing tale imaginable!

- *The Afterdark Princess* by Annie Dalton (shortlisted for the Carnegie Medal) is a good read for older children. Joe Quail is an anxious boy who is easily worried by things. When Alice comes to babysit she gives him moonglasses and shows him the Kingdom of the Afterdark. Joe finds the hero in himself when he is called upon to save the last princess of the Afterdark.

- Other similar books by Annie Dalton are *The Dream Snatcher* and *The Midnight Museum*.

# What are images?

**Draw something that comes from your imagination**

## Talking cats

### Let's imagine!

Imagine that you have a pet cat that can talk. This cat would like to know all the things that you do on school days. Make a list of (or draw) everything that you have to remember to do. Start your list with 'I wake up'.

You didn't have to wait until you had done each thing again before you wrote it, did you? You just imagined what you do each day.

Time to stretch your imagination a bit further.

Imagine that your pet wants to tell humans what it's like to be a cat.

What would it tell you? What does it like to do? What does it hate doing? What is it good at? What would it most like to happen? What does it think is the best thing about being a cat?

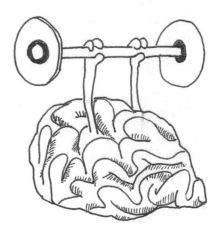

Close your eyes so that you can really begin to str-e-tch your imagination while you imagine having a conversation with your cat.

When you are ready, use a big piece of paper to draw or write about what you imagined.

## Feeling good about being me

Feeling good about who you are is really important.

There are lots of things that happen to us and around us that help us to feel OK about ourselves, but sometimes things happen that are not so nice, and then we might end up feeling bad about ourselves.

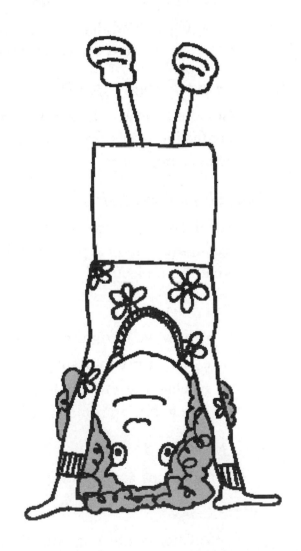

We might start to think 'I can't do this', or 'I'm no good at this', or 'Everyone has more friends than me'.

If this happens, then your imagination can help you to feel better about yourself again – *and* it can help you to actually get to *be* better at doing some of the hard things.

57

## Chapter 6

# Feelings

By doing the activities in this section you will be helping your child to:

- understand that there are no 'right' or 'wrong' feelings
- recognise how emotions can affect our bodies
- understand that feelings can change and that we can have some control over them.

### 1. How many feelings? (p.63)

Complete the activity sheet together. Instead of writing the words you could cut out feeling words from magazines and add to the list whenever your child comes across a new word.

### 2. Show me how you feel

Stand opposite each other and take turns to jump forward and show different feelings (by physical posture and facial expression). The other person tries to copy what this looks like.

*Talk about:*

- how we recognise feelings in ourselves and others
- why it is important for other people to know how we feel
- when it is OK to physically show our emotions, and when it is not OK (e.g. hitting someone when we are angry).

### 3. How I feel (p.64)

Complete the activity sheet together.

*Talk about:*

- Choose a feeling and talk about whether you or another person in the family have been in a similar situation but felt something different.

- Compare all the different things that might lead to different children feeling excited or nervous.

- Different people feel different things at different times. Feelings can change – what we might once have been nervous about, we might eventually come to enjoy or to feel more confident about.

- Point out any feelings that are similar in the family. ('It sounds as though most of us get excited when _____.' 'Almost everyone feels nervous when _____.' 'Dad and you both feel disappointed when _____.')

## 4. If feelings were colours (p.65)

Ask your child to draw a happy picture. Start with a brief discussion about how different feelings could be thought of as different colours (for example, 'I'm the colour blue today because I feel calm'; 'I'm the colour blue today because I feel sad'; 'I'm the colour red because I feel full of energy'). Ask your child what colour she would be today and why she would be that colour.

*Talk about:*

- What colour is anger? Does anger have different colours according to the intensity of the feeling?

- We can feel like a different colour at different times on different days.

- Two people could feel like the same colour for completely different reasons.

- Feelings can change very quickly, perhaps because of something that happens to us, or something that we see or hear. Is it easy to change from one 'mood' or feeling to another? When might that happen?

- We all feel unhappy, grumpy, etc., at times. This is normal. Because our moods change, that means that uncomfortable feelings, as well as nice feelings, will change, stop, or fade away gradually.

- Sometimes we can't work out why we are feeling something. Noticing an unpleasant feeling and telling someone about it can help us to cope with it, even if we don't want to talk about it in any depth.

## 5. Being in balance

Some children can find it very hard to cope when their feelings change too frequently or too quickly. Take turns to think of ideas for what you can both do to keep feelings balanced.

For example, if I keep getting angry I can:

- tell someone that I'm feeling angry

- sit and do a quiet activity until I feel more calm
- go and scribble in an 'angry book'
- write down all the things that I'm angry about
- think about what I'm going to do later that I'm looking forward to
- daydream about the thing I'd like to happen that would mean I wasn't angry any more. 'Wouldn't it be wonderful if I could have that new computer game/stay up late/go to the park'; 'if I was invisible/a giant/an adult, I would...!'

## 6. Emotion masks

Take turns to 'pull a face' to show a strong emotion, then 'remove' the face with your hands as if it were a mask and pass it to the other person. This person 'puts on' the mask, copying the expression as accurately as possible. The second player then changes the expression and passes it back to the first person – and so on.

*Talk about:*

- Which masks did you each think that you were putting on? What emotions did you pass to each other? Did these match up? Is it possible to show an emotion with just one part of the face? Did you pass different degrees of any similar emotions to each other (e.g. happy/excited)? How do we show different degrees of emotion (e.g. by facial expression, posture, actions)?
- We can have different levels of the same feeling in different situations – like having a volume control or an intensity control. For example, we could be slightly frustrated when we make a mistake, and furious when someone accuses us of something that we didn't do.
- Sadness can be felt at different levels too. Think of as many words as possible to describe different levels of sadness. Do the same for embarrassment, worry, and feeling happy.

## 7. Acting up

Take turns to act out actions and feelings together randomly, e.g. doing the ironing sadly, eating a sandwich angrily. Guess what the other person is feeling.

*Talk about:*

- Sometimes we can be saying one thing and feeling something completely different. Does your body language sometimes 'give the game away'?
- If someone tells you they are sad but they are smiling, do you believe their words or their facial expression?

- How do you usually show that you are angry? How do you usually show that you are worried?

## 8. 'Waves on the sea' parachute game

Although parachute games are usually played in groups, you can easily adapt many of them for two to three people to play by using any large piece of material, such as a round tablecloth. Parachute games are fun for children of all ages and provide an excellent focus for outdoor play. As with any games involving the use of equipment, parachute games should be supervised by an adult at all times. Small children can easily get themselves tangled up in a large parachute – at the very least this can be a very scary experience for them.

Hold the parachute with both hands at waist level. Place a soft ball (or a few soft balls) in the middle of the parachute. Take turns to give instructions for how calm or stormy the waves on the 'sea' should be, and you and your child move the parachute accordingly, while trying to stop the soft ball from falling off.

Finish with a calm rippling of the parachute and gently lay it on the ground. Sit quietly on the edge of the 'sea'.

*Talk about:*

- Feelings can be like a stormy or a quiet sea. What happens if our feelings get out of control? How might this affect us? How might it affect other people around us?
- Difficult feelings can build and subside or can come on very suddenly and perhaps unexpectedly. Pleasant feelings come and go as well. This is normal.

## 9. What shall we do with them?

Make a list of 'difficult' feelings (e.g. anger, sadness, jealousy, frustration, being fed up). Think of ideas for what to do with these feelings (e.g. when I feel angry I can tell someone, do something active to get rid of the tension in my body, scribble in a scribble book, see activity 5 in this chapter).

*Talk about:*

- Difficult feelings come and go. Feelings don't last for ever. Just because we might feel sad or angry now, doesn't mean that we are always going to be sad or always going to be an angry person. These feelings are normal. It is good to know how to handle them.

## 10. Figure it out

Draw three or four 'gingerbread' people on a large piece of paper. Label each one with a different emotion. Take turns to add details on each picture to show what happens to us physically when we experience these emotions.

- When you look at all the figures, can you see anything that any of them have in common? What are the main differences?

- When might a feeling of nervousness be useful? What other feelings might cause similar sensations in your body (e.g. a knotted stomach could be excitement, clenched fists could be linked with determination)? How does your body feel different when you are happy? What about when you are confident? If you are anxious and you change the way your body feels (e.g. by smiling and relaxing your muscles), do you start to feel a different emotion?

## How many feelings?

It is important to know about feelings. They are a big part of who we are.

There are lots of different words that *describe* how we feel.

**Happy feelings**

Think of as many feeling words as you can. Here are a few to start you off:

**happy      sad      embarrassed      angry      excited**

Collect some more words from your friends and family by asking them how they are feeling.

How many different 'happy' feelings can you think of?

## How I feel

Having a feeling doesn't mean that you are always going to be like that.

Sam might feel shy when he goes to a new place where he doesn't know anyone, but that doesn't mean that he is always 'a shy person'. There are lots of times when Sam feels very confident.

Imagine some times when you have felt some of these feelings. Draw or write about each of the feelings listed on this page.

A time when I felt very brave was  _____

_____

I felt excited when  _____

I felt relaxed when  _____

I felt nervous when  _____

I felt angry when  _____

I felt happy when  _____

I felt disappointed when  _____

## If feelings were colours

If feeling happy were a colour, what colour would it be?

**Draw something that helps you to feel happy**

## Part Three

# Coping with Change

## Chapter 7

# Thinking about Change

By doing the activities in this section you will be helping your child to:

- understand that change is a natural part of life
- understand that she can build skills to cope with change successfully
- identify any worries and concerns about change
- build confidence for coping with change.

## 1. All change

Play an 'I Spy Change' game while you are out and about together. There will be natural changes that you can comment on, such as trees losing their leaves, or tadpoles turning into frogs, and also man-made changes such as a building being knocked down, a new building being erected, a change of window display in a shop, etc. Encourage your child to think about what has changed and what has stayed the same.

*Talk about:*

- Even when there is a big change to cope with, there will still be lots of elements of the situation or the people involved that will stay the same.
- Point out aspects of personal change linked to your observations. 'Do you remember the time when…that was great fun wasn't it?' or 'That was hard but we got through it really well because we helped each other.'

## 2. Word play

Help your child to make a list of as many words/phrases as you can both think of to do with change. For example:

> scary, exciting, worrying, interesting, challenging, funny, sad, quick, slow, controlled, uncontrolled, made by me, made by someone else, stressful, puzzling, good, horrible.

There is no need to discourage negative feelings about change at this stage. Allow your child time to explore all the possible feelings, and to feel reassured that it is normal to be worried or scared about some changes and excited about others.

## 3. What is change?

Think of one change that your child has made because he wanted to (e.g. choosing a new family pet or changing his bedroom) and one change that has happened that he had no, or little choice about (e.g. a change of school).

*Talk about:*

- What are some of the differences and similarities between the two types of change?

- Why would someone choose to make a change (e.g. because they want to feel better; because someone else suggests it; because they think they should; because they want to be like their friends)?

- What do we need to have or to know in order to make a successful change (e.g. we need to know what the change will involve; we may need help from others; we need to really want the change to work for us)?

- What makes change easier to cope with (e.g. when there are lots of people making the same change; when we have already made a similar change so we can guess what it is going to be like; when we can talk to someone about it; meeting someone from the new place; visiting a new place to have a look around)?

- What can we do to keep feeling OK about the change (e.g. reward ourselves; continue to set small goals)?

## 4. Skills for change

Draw a life path together, showing all the important changes that have taken place during your child's life. The path can be drawn metaphorically or with sketches to represent actual events. So 'starting school' might be represented by a drawing of a school building or by a mountain (it was tough going), or a sun (I loved it from the first day). This activity can highlight many different vulnerabilities and strengths, and plenty of time should be given for talking about it while your child is drawing. Possible discussion points are:

- How/why did the changes happen? What was good about each change? What was not so good?

- What did you/your child learn? Did you both feel the same about each of the changes?

- What helped your child to cope? What skills have you both developed by coping with change?
- Did one change lead to others? What stayed the same?

## 5. Quick draw

Ask your child to draw the stages of one change that she has already coped with successfully. This could be a big change, such as moving house, or a small change, such as starting to do regular exercise. Start with a picture of how things used to be. Draw a second picture that shows how things are now. Then draw a third picture, showing how these changes happened.

*Talk about:*

- What were the steps that helped you to make the change?
- What did you need to know or have in order to make the change?
- What was the best bit about making the change? What was the worst bit?
- What are you most pleased about now that you have coped with the change?

Your child might find it helpful to compare her experience with yours – but remember that your adult coping strategies may not necessarily be the most appropriate ones for her to use.

## 6. Big and small

Talk about the differences between big and small changes. What sort of changes are scary? What sort of changes are fun?

## 7. Experiments

Experiment with 'change' within the family. For example, everyone tastes a new food that they've never tried before, or plays a new game together, or watches something on television that they wouldn't normally watch. Talk about how easy or difficult it is to make these sorts of changes. Are there any benefits?

Change one thing that you usually do without thinking about it (a habit). What does this feel like? (For example, if you are right-handed, can you hold your toast in your left hand? Can you sit in a different position while you are reading or watching TV (e.g. legs uncrossed)? For how long can you remember to do this? How easy or difficult is it to make these sorts of changes? Are there any benefits?)

## 8. Confidence for change (1)

Ask at least three different people what they think confidence means.

*Talk about:*

- Confidence can mean different things to different people.
- Some people can appear to be very confident when they are not really. Most of us are confident in some things we do and in some places. We might need to build up our confidence with other things.
- Think of one thing that you would like to be able to do with more confidence.

## 9. Help the wizard and Grimes to solve the riddle (p.75)

Search for the letters in the riddle that make up the word 'confidence'.

## 10. Confidence for change (2)

Ask your child to imagine someone who he thinks is very confident. This might be a TV personality or a fictional character or someone he knows. Make a list together of all the things that this person does that causes them to appear confident. Be as specific as possible. If your child says 'They look confident', then talk about how the person stands, walks, sits, dresses, their facial expression, etc. If he says 'They sound confident', talk about how they sound – fast? slow? loud? quiet? somewhere in between? And so on.

Encourage him to rehearse/role-play a difficult situation with you (such as meeting new people) as if he were the confident person that he was thinking of. Talk about how that feels.

## 11. Let's imagine (p.76)

Read the confidence imagework to your child and then ask her to draw a picture of her confident image.

## Confidence

Close your eyes and take three full breaths to help you to feel relaxed. As you breathe out the first breath, relax your shoulders… As you breathe out the second breath, relax your arms… As you breathe out the third time, relax your fingers…

Ask your imagination to give you an image that somehow shows us what it's like to be confident. The image could be an animal, a plant or an object – anything at all. Just close your eyes and see what your imagination comes up with.

Can you picture it in your mind? What can you see? Have a good look at the image and tell me all about it.

Now imagine that you are this image. Step into being this image of confidence… Take your time and really feel what this is like… What do you look like?… Do you move? How do you move?… Do you make a noise? What noises do you make?…

What do you think about?… What are the nice things about being this image of confidence?… Is there anything that is not so nice?…

Where do you live?… Who are your friends?… What do you do best?… What is the most important thing about you?…

If you could give some advice to children about being confident, what would you tell them?

When you have found out everything you can about being confident, come back to being you again. Thank your imagination for showing you this image… Let the image gradually fade away…

Remember that you can always call up the image again in the future if you want to remind yourself what it feels like to be as confident as this…

Come back to being in the room again… Have a bit of a stretch and open your eyes…

When you are ready, draw or write about what it's like to be confident.

*Talk about:*

- How did the image of confidence move? What did it feel like to be so confident? Relate this to how we can act in a confident way even when we are feeling a bit unsure.

- What were the positive things about being this image? Was there anything that didn't feel comfortable or that felt unhelpful?

- What is the opposite of feeling confident? Draw pictures to represent this opposite. Compare this with the confidence image and think about the differences.

- Think of a time when you have already felt as confident as this. What was happening? How did you know that you felt confident? What could you feel in your body? What were you thinking about? Draw a picture to show what was happening when you felt confident (p.77).

## 12. Story treasures (3)

There are plenty of children's books about confidence and feeling OK about yourself. These are some that I have used, which are suitable for ages 7–11 years:

- *Scaredy Cat* by Anne Fine. Poppy is afraid of ghosts and monsters but needs to find a way of showing her classmates that she is not a 'scaredy-cat'.

- *Only a Show* by Anne Fine. Anna is worried about doing a five-minute show for her class. She is worried that she isn't confident, clever or funny, and that she can't do anything 'special'. In the end, her show is a triumph.

- *I'm Scared* by Bel Mooney. A book exploring some of the things that young children are often afraid of. Kitty is afraid of the dark, but she is able to come to the rescue when other children are afraid of things.

- *Fergus the Forgetful* by Margaret Ryan and Wendy Smith. Fergus can never remember things like taking his PE kit or his homework to school, but he is a mine of information about 'important' things and manages to help his school win a quiz.

## Help the wizard and Grimes to solve the riddle

Long, long ago in magical times, there lived a wizard and a cat called Grimes.

They lived in the forest on the mountain slopes and wove their magic out of wishes and hopes.

They knew that the mountain had a secret to tell – a magic much greater than the wizard's best spell.

But neither Grimes nor the wizard knew where to begin to look for the secret – without? or within?

Then one day an ant came to visit the pair – a wise little ant with a secret to share.

'I may not be big, I can't swim or jump high, I'm not very strong and I can't even fly,

but I know that a clue to the magic that's here can be found, if you look, at the start of a cheer,

at the start of ourselves, at the start of each night, at the beginning of friendships and some impish delight,

at the start of excitement, at the end of some fun, add the middle of peaceful, and now I have done.'

'This', said the ant, 'is one thing that I've found by talking and sharing and trying things out.'

## Lets imagine

Draw your image
of confidence

**Draw a picture of a time when you have felt confident**

## Chapter 8

# Preparing for Change

By doing the activities in this section you will be helping your child to:

- understand the need to prepare for changes and challenges
- recognise how some changes can be broken down into small steps.

## 1. Involvement

If there is a specific change coming up soon, begin to talk about it in concrete terms. Name and describe the change. Involve your child in family discussions about what will happen. Try to include him in part of the decision-making, for example choosing colours for his new room, preparing his school uniform. One of the most important strategies for helping your child to cope with change is to involve him in the process as much as possible. Allowing him to have some sense of control over even a small part of a change can help to take away some of the anxiety about the 'unknown'.

## 2. Prepare to dive! (p.81)

Complete the activity sheet together.

*Talk about:*

- the importance of preparing for new or difficult things
- some ways in which we can research what we might need to know or have so that we feel prepared for changes.

## 3. I packed my suitcase

Think of a variety of different activities or adventures that would need different equipment and clothing (for example, mountaineering, deep sea diving, going to an adventure playground, visiting a hot country, visiting a cold country, going on a treasure hunt).

Choose one of these and play a round of 'I packed my suitcase and I took…' Each of you has to remember what has already been packed and add one more item to the list. When the list gets too long to remember, choose another adventure and start again.

Anyone can challenge the inclusion of an item that doesn't seem relevant for the particular adventure.

*Talk about:*

- How can we prepare ourselves for adventures and challenges?
- If we think something is going to be scary, embarrassing or difficult, what could we do to help ourselves to cope with this?

## 4. Research

Talk with someone who has already made a similar change. How did he or she cope? What helped? What didn't help?

## 5. Imagine making a change (p.82)

Complete the activity sheet together.

*Talk about:*

- Imagining that you have already achieved a goal can be more powerful than planning what you will have to do beforehand. Athletes are often trained to see themselves having made the perfect high jump, having achieved their personal best time, and so on.
- Our imagination can help us to cope with things successfully. If we imagine something clearly enough, we create a memory – as if it had actually happened. The details may turn out to be quite different, but the feeling (e.g. confidence, excitement) can be the same.

## 6. Steps along the way (p.83)

It is important for your child to recognise the benefits of taking things 'one step at a time' and, as he begins to make changes and achieve his goals, to give himself a 'pat on the back'.

Use a diary, wall calendar or the 'Steps' activity sheet to mark the stages of preparation for a particular change. Colour in the steps as they are completed. Make sure that each step is well defined and is small enough to be manageable (but not too small, so that you end up with too many steps/stages and risk your child losing motivation).

### 7. *Explore*

Begin to collect information specific to the change. For example, help your child to research her new school or the new house. Many schools now offer 'virtual' tours on their websites. Use an atlas or a map to locate the school or house. If possible, visit the area or the new school before the move and take photos.

### 8. *Reassure*

Talk with your child about how he will find out the important things about whatever change is going to happen. This might include the rules, procedures, timetables, etc., for his new school. Reassure him that he will be told what happens at lunchtime and breaks, for example. If your child is particularly anxious about a school transition, try to find out about induction days at the new school. What sort of thing can your child expect to happen on these days? Is there a reward/merit system in place at the new school?

### 9. *Acknowledge and celebrate*

If you are moving to a new area, or your child's friend is moving away, help him to acknowledge and celebrate the friendship(s). Make cards for friends; set up a friendship blog. Reassure your child that moving away doesn't always have to mean the end of a friendship.

## Prepare to dive!

When you look after yourself, you feel more ready to enjoy the easy, exciting or fun things in life, and more ready to cope with those things that are especially difficult.

It's a bit like being ready to go diving in the sea.

Think about what you would need to have with you and what you would need to know if you were going diving.

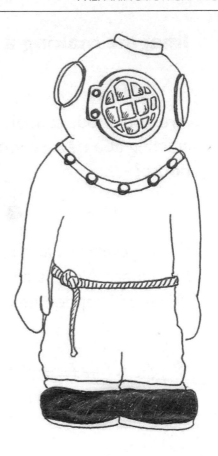

Before I go diving I would need to be: _____

_____

_____


I would need to have: _____

_____

_____


I would need to know: _____

_____

_____

## Imagine making a change

Are you about to make a change like starting at a new school or moving house?

Close your eyes and imagine that the change has already happened. What is different? What is happening? How do you feel? What will happen next? Draw or write about the change.

## Steps along the way

One thing I'd like to be able to do is: _____

_____

These are the steps I need to take:

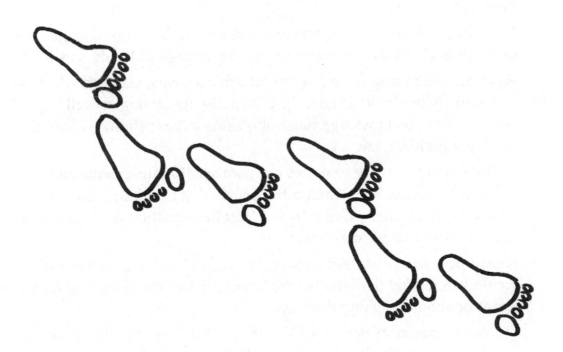

*Chapter9*

# Making a Change

Following the suggestions in this section will help you and your child to:

- minimise the effects of any stress involved in change
- recognise successes
- consolidate skills.

## 1. The 6 'R's

In order to help your child to maintain progress, use the 6 'R's: *routine, revisit, record, remind, retell, resist.*

- **Routine:** during times of change try to maintain as many familiar routines as possible (e.g. bedtime and mealtimes). Keep other changes to a minimum.

- **Revisit:** think about using one of the strategies for stress management outlined in Part Four, or revisit one of the strategies already used.

- **Record**: continue to keep a record of achievements, using the flags, stars or badges (Chapter 4, activity 7). Give praise for strategies well remembered. Acknowledge times of making a 'wise choice', times of solving a problem, etc.

  Talk about learning to notice our own small achievements and praising ourselves. Sometimes other people don't notice or don't know how we feel or what we've achieved. Just because they don't praise us doesn't mean that we didn't do well.

- **Remind:** invite your child to draw 'me before' and 'me afterwards' pictures to remind her how far she has come. List the skills that have been learnt or enhanced along the way.

  Make a poster or design a TV advert called 'Your family needs you!' to highlight the invaluable part your child plays in the family just by being her.

- **Retell:** make up a story together about how a child or animal has coped with change, tell a familiar story of how someone in the past (e.g. a grandparent) has coped with adversity or simply retell a sequence of events related to the actual change with which your child is coping, emphasising a positive aspect: 'Do you remember when we first talked about your new school? That was the day that you showed me how to find a map on the internet, and then we worked out how far away the school was from our house. Do you remember what you said?…'

- **Resist:** don't be tempted to set new goals too quickly. Give your child time to enjoy what he has achieved.

## 2. Check in regularly

Discuss any new worries and achievements as they come up. Set aside a specific time to 'check in'. Try to negotiate this time with your child to start with, and then eventually leave it up to her to check in with you if she feels she needs to. Make sure that she knows that you are always keen to hear how things are going.

## 3. Get creative

Create a collage or a scrapbook of all the things that happen because of the change. (Include both positive and difficult aspects.)

## 4. Encourage friendships

Actively promote new friendships, especially if the change has involved a move to a new area. Investigate other friendship opportunities for your child outside school.

## 5. Keep things in proportion

Ups and downs are a natural part of any change process. Your child may well have days when he feels confused, sad or anxious, despite all your efforts to prepare him for change. Don't let these difficult times grow out of proportion. They are just a signal that he needs a helping hand. Acknowledge the reality of his feelings. Remind him that he has coped with difficult times before and that the feelings will pass.

Remember, too, that it's OK to miss something and talk about how things used to be. (This is not the same as constantly 'living in the past'.) Missing something that's gone doesn't prevent you from enjoying something new.

## 6. Model the desired response

There is no substitute for being a good role model for your child. In difficult situations try to stay calm and verbalise your strategies for coping: 'I am feeling a bit confused. I am going to make a list of all the things we need to do.'

Look after yourself in whatever way you know works best for you. Remember, your child will learn effective coping strategies from watching those around her.

## 7. Seek support

If you find that your child's distress is acute, ask your GP or practice nurse about the help that is available, or speak to your child's teacher. There is always plenty that can be done and there is no need to struggle on your own.

*Part Four*

# Coping with stress

# Chapter 10

# What is Stress?

By doing the activities in this section you will be helping your child to:

- understand why our bodies might react to 'false alarms'
- recognise the signs of stress
- understand that there are different types of stress
- understand that the way we think about a situation can affect how stressed we feel.

## 1. Meet the brain (p.93)

Colour in the different parts of the brain and talk about the function of each of the areas. It is important for children to have some basic understanding of what happens in the brain and how this affects how they feel. (See p.22.)

*Talk about:*
When you are feeling very stressed your brain is sending signals to your body to help you to run away or to fight. This can be really useful if you are in a dangerous situation, but not useful if you are just thinking about something horrible happening, or you are getting worried about a test or about being late for school or not being able to find your favourite T-shirt. Your body gets full of 'stress' chemicals and this might make you feel angry or tired or very 'wobbly'.

If this happens, then you can help your body to calm down again by doing exercise (like running or cycling or just going for a walk), or by doing a relaxation and thinking about something nice. Then your brain sends different signals to the rest of your body so that 'feel good' chemicals are released. These will help you to feel more in control and more calm.

## 2. Stressed out!

Make a list of five situations which you find stressful, and five situations that you think your child finds stressful.

Ask your child to think of five things that he finds worrying or stressful.

*Talk about:*

- Have you each come up with different *types* of stress? An example of an emotional stress would be difficulties within a friendship. A physical trigger to stress might be continuous loud noise, or being in a crowded room. Mental stress might be something like studying for a test.
- What are the similarities and differences in the lists that you and your child made?

## 3. Some stress can be good for you (p.94)

Think about times when a reasonable amount of stress can be useful. Help your child to make a list or draw times when 'a bit of stress' has helped him to achieve something.

## 4. Feelings (p.95)

Complete the activity sheet together. Sometimes children don't know what emotion they are feeling, or why they are feeling a bit 'churned up'. Understanding more about how their body works can help them to recognise early warning signs and take action to check out their concerns.

*Talk about:*

- what happens to our bodies when we are in a stressful situation
- how our body can react with 'false alarms' – we are just thinking worry thoughts, but the body thinks we are in danger
- how our imagination can cause the same reactions even when the situation has passed or when we are thinking about what *might* happen.

## 5. Different ways of thinking

What would each of you do with a blank piece of paper and a pencil (e.g. write a story, make a paper aeroplane, draw a picture, write a list of 'things to do')?

*Talk about:*

- A group of people who are each given a piece of blank paper and a pencil but no instructions as to what to do with them will probably have very different feelings about it – for example, *panic* ('I don't know what to do'; 'I'm no good at deciding'; 'I can't think up good ideas'; 'I know that whatever I do will be wrong'); *enthusiasm* ('I can do anything that I want'; 'I've got loads of good ideas'; 'I love the freedom of experimenting'); or *anxiety* disguised as anger ('How am I expected to know what she wants?'; 'What does she think I am – a mind-reader?'; 'She just wants to keep me quiet for a while'; 'This is really boring'). These feelings do not have anything to do with the task itself, it is our thoughts *about* a task that affect how we feel and what we do in such situations.

- Different people might see the same things in different ways. Two people seeing a fight in the playground are likely to remember different details, depending on where they were standing and maybe depending on how well they know or like the people involved. One perception is not necessarily better or more 'right' than another – there are just different ways of looking at things, and this will be largely dependent on our past experiences and knowledge.

## 6. Feeling tense and feeling relaxed

Read the 'What's it like?' imagework exercise to your child.

## What's it like?

Perhaps you have noticed that there are times when people might be feeling one thing but acting as though they are feeling something completely different.

Sometimes our feelings get all mixed up.

So let's think a bit more about what our bodies feel like when we have different emotions.

Think of a time when you felt a bit upset or cross about something. I bet your body felt very stiff and perhaps you felt a bit churned up inside? This is called tension.

If tension was an animal or a plant or anything else, what would it be?…

Close your eyes and imagine something that somehow shows us what it's like to be tense…

Imagine that you can become your image of tension… Step into being this plant or animal or object… What do you feel like when you are this image?

What does your body feel like?… What is the worst thing about being this image?… Feel a frown growing from deep inside you… Feel it spreading all the way through you… Really notice what this is like…

Now step out of being this image and back to being you… Give yourself a shake all over…shake your hands, shake your arms, shake your body, shake your legs! Let all that tension disappear…

Draw or write about your image of tension on a big piece of paper. When you have finished, we'll do the next bit of imagining…

When we are not tense, our body feels more relaxed.

If the feeling of relaxing was an animal, a plant or an object, what would it be?

Close your eyes and take three deep breaths, letting the air out slowly as you breathe out… Ask your imagination to come up with an image that somehow shows us what it's like to be relaxed… It could be an object, a plant or an animal… Whatever it is, just let the image appear…

When you are ready, imagine that you can become your image of relaxation…

Step into being this animal or plant or object and really feel what it's like…
What does your body feel like?…

Feel a smile grow from deep inside you… Feel it spreading all the way through you… Really notice what this is like…

What is the best thing about being this image?…

Spend some time just being this image and enjoying the feelings… When you are ready, step out of this image and back to being you. Open your eyes slowly and have a stretch and a yawn!

On a large piece of paper, draw or write about your feelings of being relaxed.

*Talk about:*

- The different physical sensations that we produce in our body when we are relaxed.

- What does it feel like to be tense and what does it feel like to be very relaxed? Notice the difference between being very tense, and feeling strong without feeling excessive tension.

- Why is it important for our bodies to be relaxed sometimes?

- Is there such a thing as useful tension? When do we need to be tense? Are there times when you have tension in your body that doesn't need to be there?

## 7. Snowmen

Start by imagining that you are both newly built snowmen. Stand very still with your arms by your sides. Make all your muscles tense. Now imagine the sun has come out and it is getting warmer and warmer. The snowmen start to 'melt' until they are pools of melted snow on the floor. Flop gently onto the floor. Lie very still, letting all your muscles go floppy. Now the snow clouds come and lots of snow falls so that you can be built up into snowmen again. Stand tall and stiff. Melt once more. Then go back to being you again. Stand up tall and shake your arms, hands and legs as if you are shaking the snow off.

## Meet the brain

This is what the brain looks like from one side. The diagram shows just some of the many functions of each part.

Front of the head                                    Back of the head

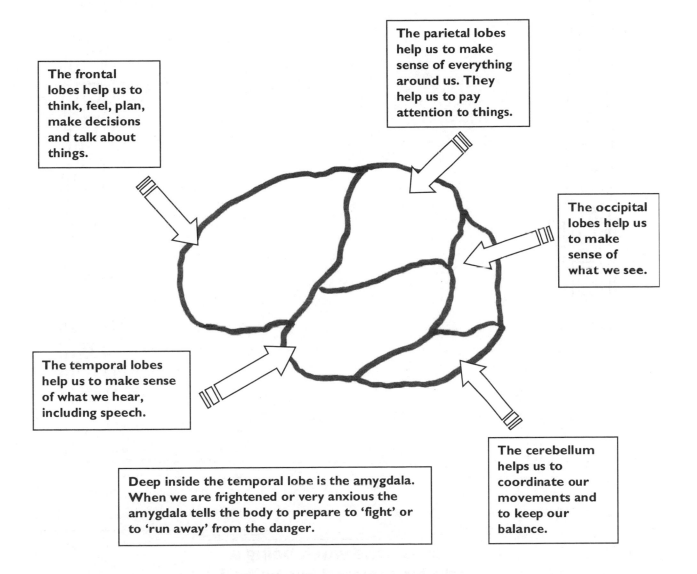

The frontal lobes help us to think, feel, plan, make decisions and talk about things.

The parietal lobes help us to make sense of everything around us. They help us to pay attention to things.

The occipital lobes help us to make sense of what we see.

The temporal lobes help us to make sense of what we hear, including speech.

The cerebellum helps us to coordinate our movements and to keep our balance.

Deep inside the temporal lobe is the amygdala. When we are frightened or very anxious the amygdala tells the body to prepare to 'fight' or to 'run away' from the danger.

## Some stress can be good for you

Draw a time when being a little bit stressed has helped you to do something

## Feelings

Have you ever worried about something that hasn't happened yet? What did your body feel like? Tick the feelings that you get when you are worried.

| | | | |
|---|---|---|---|
| butterflies in my tummy | ☐ | heart beats faster | ☐ |
| headache | ☐ | fidget a lot | ☐ |
| feel sick | ☐ | can't think clearly | ☐ |
| tight muscles | ☐ | wobbly knees | ☐ |

Can you think of any other feelings that you might get when you are worried?

Have you ever got excited about something long before it happened? What did your body feel like then?

Your imagination can make your body feel different things. Sometimes this is good, but sometimes this is not useful for you.

Sometimes you can change what you are imagining so that you can *feel* better.

**Imagine that!**

*Chapter 11*

# Changing how we Feel

By doing the activities in this section you will be helping your child to:
- understand that he can change the way he copes with stress
- experiment with lots of different ways to deal with the effects of stress
- identify the strategies that work best for him.

## 1. Relaxed breathing

Sit in a comfortable chair or stand in front of a full length mirror. Place one hand lightly on your chest and the other hand just below your bottom ribs. Breathe in fully and deeply, watching what happens. Which hand moves the most? Do your shoulders rise? Does your stomach move in or out? Does your posture change in any way? Now breathe out and note any changes again.

Ideally, your child will have felt his stomach move downwards and outwards when he breathed in, with only slight movement in his chest. His shoulders will hardly have moved at all, and his posture will have remained balanced. This is *diaphragmatic* breathing. If your child raised his shoulders and expanded his chest or pulled in his stomach as he took a deep breath, he was not breathing in a relaxed way. Diaphragmatic breathing is very natural but may take a while to relearn if a child's breathing pattern has changed over the years. Once children are able to direct their attention to the diaphragm, they will notice themselves taking relaxing deep breaths during the day, and this will help them to feel calm. Suggest to your child that he can consciously take two or three relaxed breaths to help control any feelings of anxiety before these get too big.

## 2. Build a 'refuelling station'

Make a special place for your child to go when she needs time out to unwind and 'fill up' with good feelings. For example, this could be a story den made with blankets or sheets, a cosy armchair filled with lots of cushions, or a giant teddy to cuddle. Using this place regularly will mean that at other times she can also imagine that she is there, in order to feel the same sense of calm.

### 3. Get messy

Enjoy some messy play together without restraint! Sand play, water play, painting or mud play can be a great way to relieve tension for some children. If your child finds messy play difficult to engage in, try dancing to 'happy' music instead.

### 4. Massage

Give your child a back massage.

Ask his permission first. (It is important for children to be able to say 'no', even to the offer of a relaxing massage.) Silently massage his back, neck and shoulders for two minutes. Now swap and let him massage your back for two minutes. When the time is up, remember to thank each other.

### 5. Humour

Make up a nonsense song or a funny poem about change. Humour is a great stress buster and a boost to self-esteem.

*Talk about:*

- Sometimes laughing can help us to feel more relaxed. When might this be appropriate? When would it not be appropriate?
- Have you ever felt upset or angry about something that you could laugh about later?
- What makes you laugh? What makes your friend laugh?

### 6. Pass a smile

This is a fun group game but can also be played with just two people.

Players sit in a circle. Everyone tries to look very solemn. A child is chosen to start off a smile. He sends a smile to the person sitting next to him. This person smiles, then 'zips' his or her lips in order to 'hold' the smile before turning to the next person and unzipping the smile to pass it on! When the smile has been around the circle once, the group has a go at passing another smile, this time even more quickly.

*Talk about:*

- It is sometimes possible to have control over how we feel.
- How does your body feel when you smile? What makes you smile? Can you tell the difference between a real smile and a pretend one, or an 'unkind' smile? How can you tell the difference?

### 7. Giggle switch

Choose who is A and who is B. Person A tries to make person B giggle in any way they can without touching them. Person B must keep eye contact and try to keep a straight face. At any time you can say 'giggle switch' and swap roles.

*Talk about:*

- The importance of laughter.
- How do you feel when you have had a 'fit of the giggles'? Talk about the difference between 'laughing *at* someone' and 'laughing *with* someone'. Laughter can have very different qualities and can therefore cause us to feel quite differently too.

### 8. Musical drawing

Draw whatever comes to mind while listening to a selection of music that has different rhythms and moods.

*Talk about:*

- Music can affect our mood. Is there a piece of music that always makes you feel sad or always makes you feel happy?
- Is there some music that you could listen to that would help you to feel calm when you've had a stressful day?

### 9. Fidget flop

This can be done at any time as a quick way to release tension, or as an introduction to an activity that requires a lot of concentration.

Imagine that your fingers are all animals or people and they're having a pretend play-fight. Make them play at fighting each other. Get them tangled up and then untangle them again… Now let them slowly stop, and then make them float instead. Let your fingers float around each other without touching…and now gently stroke your fingers across each other… Now have them fight each other again. They're moving faster and faster… Gradually they slow down… Can you feel them tingling? Let your fingers gently float around each other again. Sometimes, if you do this gently and slowly enough, you will be able to feel the energy between your fingers, even though they are not touching. It feels like a tickle or like stroking silk. Can you feel that?… Have a little play with this energy. Imagine that you are holding a ball of energy… Feel the size of the ball. Move your hands closer together and further apart, all the time noticing the feel of the energy ball between them… Now let your hands flop down, as though they've gone to sleep.

## 10. When I want to calm myself

Gently close your eyes and feel yourself relaxing. When you breathe in, you can feel a relaxing, warm feeling filling up your body. Each time you breathe out, you are breathing away all the tightness in your muscles that you don't need. Feel the air as it very slowly goes in and out of you… Imagine that there is a yellow light which is coming up from beneath your feet. It moves through your feet…your legs…your body…your arms…your shoulders…and your head…and it goes through the top of your head and floats away… So now you feel very relaxed, but still wide awake and able to…[add whatever it is that your child needs to do next].

## 11. A focus relaxation

This type of relaxation works by focusing the mind on different areas of the body and just being aware of what that area feels like. Often, if we try to relax, we try too hard! In our efforts to relax we actually set up more tension. In observing what the body is doing, there is a natural tendency simply to allow any areas of tension to relax and release. This relaxation can be done lying down or seated.

- Make sure there are no distractions. Take the phone off the hook and switch off mobile phones.
- Check that the room temperature feels comfortable. Have a blanket or duvet handy. Some children like the extra comfort of this if they are going to relax deeply.
- Remember, the next thing that you do after a relaxation should be very calm and slow.
- Read each part very slowly and calmly, with plenty of pauses to allow your child time to follow your instructions.

Sometimes if we are very anxious or nervous or tense about something, it shows in our body. Our muscles become tight. Maybe they begin to ache a little bit. We might feel 'knotted up' inside. This can feel very uncomfortable. It's a really nice feeling to be able to relax your body…and it will help you to feel confident and more able to do things that are a bit difficult.

When you are ready, let your eyes close gently and settle yourself into a comfortable position.

Notice the feel of your body on the floor [in the chair]… Now start to notice your feet… Put all your attention on your feet and really notice what they feel like. Maybe they feel warm or cold; perhaps they are numb or itchy…tight or relaxed. Just notice whatever you can feel in your feet…

Now gently move your thoughts from your feet to the lower part of your legs. Let your thoughts leave your feet and just move very easily to your legs. Notice whatever feeling is there just at this moment… There are no right or wrong feelings… Whatever you can feel is OK…

Now move up to your knees…and then the top part of your legs, and notice whatever feelings are there… Now start to notice your tummy, feel what's happening when you breathe gently in and out… Start to think about your shoulders…feel any tightness just melt away… Notice all the feelings around your neck and your head…

Let your thoughts go gently to your back…all along the length of your back…feel the relaxation spreading through your body… Thinking about your arms now…just notice whatever is there…and down the length of your arms into your hands… Notice all your fingers, one by one. Whatever is there, just notice it…

Now, instead of thinking of yourself in parts, feel your whole body relax. Just letting go…letting the floor [chair] support you, and just relaxing into it… As you breathe in, breathe in relaxation…and feel it spreading through every part of you… As you breathe out, feel your body relaxing even more… breathing in…and out…like waves on a sea shore… Lie quietly for a few moments and enjoy the feeling of being relaxed…

[Allow at least one or two minutes of quietness.]

Keep noticing your body, and start to listen to whatever sounds there are around you… Begin to move your hands and feet a little bit… When you feel ready, open your eyes and look around you… Lie or sit quietly for a short while before stretching and having a yawn.

## 12. Just hanging loose!

This is a slightly different version of the preceding focus relaxation and could also be done at bedtime to help restful sleep.

Find a really comfortable position to sit [lie] in, ready to let your whole body go loose… Let your body sink into the chair or cushion [bed] so that now you are as still as can be… Begin to think about your toes. Relax your toes and feel them getting warm and heavy… Let all the tightness just float away from your toe muscles so that they are not having to do any extra work… Now let go of any tightness in your legs. Put all your attention into your legs and let the muscles relax, release, let go…

When your legs are relaxed, begin to think about your tummy. Feel the muscles in your tummy go soft, relaxing and releasing any tightness that might have been there… Feel your hands and arms getting warm and heavy as they rest comfortably by your sides… Your fingers are very slightly curled, but there is no tightness in them…

Now think about your shoulders. Gently raise your shoulders up towards your ears and feel how the muscles have to work to keep them there... Then let go...and feel the difference... Notice how it felt when they were tight and how it feels when your shoulders are more relaxed... Now let go even more than you thought you could...

Think about your face. Feel a smile starting to come... Let the smile spread and spread until it reaches your eyes... Now let go, so that all the muscles on your face gently relax and your forehead feels a little wider and higher than it did before...

Notice your breathing. Be very still as you feel the air going into your body when you breathe gently and quietly... Feel it as it slowly goes out again... In and out, like waves on the seashore... In...and...out...in...and...out...

Now forget about your breathing and just feel yourself relaxing more and more... Stay like this for a little while and imagine a special place that you like to be.

After a little while you will be ready to [fall asleep/do the next thing].

## 13. Taking care of myself every day (p.102)

Make a list together of 'ways to look after myself'. This list might include such things as going for a walk, relaxing in a deep bath, having a 'quiet time', playing with my dog/cat, having a hug, etc. Try to get at least 20 items on the list.

Help your child to choose up to three things that he will do when he is feeling worried, fed up or tired during the next week. Be specific – for example, 'When I notice signs of stress', or 'When I notice myself getting up tight or upset, I will go for a bike ride, relax on my bed; take some time for myself, play with the dog, talk to a friend, ask Mummy for a hug.'

*Talk about:*

- Contrast different ways in which people (children and adults) choose to relax. Highlight the need to unwind in some way when things have been very busy.
- Talk about mental and emotional 'busyness' as well as physical 'busyness'. Highlight the importance of physical activity as one way to relax the mind.

## 14. How to make my perfect day (p.103)

Encourage imaginative answers. Giving children their wishes in fantasy can be a great way of relieving pent-up frustration.

## Taking care of myself every day

Imagine that you've had a very busy day at school and you feel quite tired.

Think of all the things that you could do now to help yourself to feel relaxed and refreshed. Draw or write about them here.

## How to make my perfect day

Imagine that you have had the most perfect day. Draw what happened.

*Part Five*

# Coping with Anxiety

*Note:* The following activities refer to worries as distinct from anxiety, in order to show children that it is 'normal' to have concerns about things, but that sometimes our worries can take over and dominate our thinking and behaviour.

## Chapter 12

# Thinking, Feeling, Doing

By doing the activities in this section you will be helping your child to:

- learn how to recognise and monitor patterns of feelings and thoughts
- explore the idea that worries come in different shapes and sizes.

## 1. Mixing it up

A variation of 'Simon says':

Demonstrate movements for your child to follow, such as 'stand on one leg, touch your ear, wave, clap'. When the instruction is 'do this', then you both do the movement. When the instruction is 'do that', you make the movement but your child should stand still.

*Talk about:*

- Is it easy or difficult to listen, think and do something all at the same time? What could make it easier?
- When we repeat a behaviour often enough, we begin not to think about it any more. Why is this useful? When might it not be useful?
- Sometimes our thoughts become automatic too. Automatic thoughts can sometimes be useful – they can save us thinking time! But if they are negative or unhelpful thoughts then we can learn to recognise these and can begin to take control of them (see other activities in this section).

## 2. Junk thoughts (p.110)

Complete the activity sheet together.

Think of some unhelpful thoughts first, and then some helpful ones to use before, during and after a difficult situation. It is important that your child chooses his own words for these. What works best for you may not necessarily be what works best for him.

*Talk about:*

This can be explained in terms of eating healthy food and 'junk' food. When we think thoughts like 'I'm hopeless' or 'I can't do this' or 'No one will speak to me', this is like eating 'junk food'. These thoughts affect us in a negative way.

When we have thoughts like 'I can learn how to do this' or 'This might be difficult but I'm going to have a go', 'It doesn't matter if I make a mistake, so long as I try my best', 'I know how to be a good friend', then this is like eating healthy food, and these thoughts are good for us.

## 3. Just because

This game is fun to play with just two people and can easily be adapted for more players. Player One describes a very simple event such as 'The dog barked'. Player Two gives a reason: 'because it saw a cat'. Player One gives a possible consequence: 'The postman dropped all the letters'. Player Two then starts with a new event. Players try to give the causes and effects as quickly as possible, and can be challenged by the other person if their answers are thought not to be relevant.

Exploring cause and effect helps children to appreciate how one action can lead to another, how an event can be caused by several different 'triggers', and how feelings can occur for many different reasons.

## 4. Catching thoughts (p.111)

Complete the activity sheet together. Take turns to think up ideas about what to do with the worry thought in the net.

*Talk about:*

- Thoughts cause worried feelings, not the actual events.

## 5. Good news and bad news

Player one starts off with a piece of 'good' news. The next person adds 'but the bad news is…' For example: 'The good news is that school is closed for the day… The bad news is that we all have extra homework to do. The good news is that the homework is to write about the local funfair… The bad news is that the funfair is closed for repairs… The good news is that the owner of the funfair is giving away free ice cream… The bad news is, they don't have any cones.'

Talk about being creative in thinking up possible good news related to the 'bad' news. Have you ever been in a difficult situation that turned out to be useful for you?

## 6. Worry town

Make up a short story or a play together involving a detective who has been sent to a small town where worries have taken over all the adults. The detective interviews a teacher, a doctor, a baker, a fireman, a factory worker, a builder, etc. Each person is very worried about everything to do with their job!

*Talk about:*

Do you think everyone has worries? Do people worry about the same sorts of things? Are some worries useful? What happens when worries take up a lot of thinking time and aren't resolved?

## Junk thoughts

Sometimes our thoughts are not very helpful to us.

Having these thoughts is a bit like eating too much junk food – they make us feel bad!

Think of some things that people might say to themselves that would stop them from learning a new skill, like playing football or riding a bike. These are junk thoughts.

_____

_____

Now think up some helpful thoughts.

_____

_____

If you were going to do something that might be difficult what could you say to yourself before you start?

_____

_____

What could you say to yourself while you are in the situation?

_____

_____

What could you say to yourself afterwards?

_____

_____

## Catching thoughts

Sometimes worry thoughts come into our minds and we hardly know they are there until they start to make us feel different.

You can learn to catch those thoughts before they make mischief.

When you notice a worry thought, imagine yourself catching it so you can have a good look at it.

Now that it is in your worry net, you can see that it is just a worry thought! It doesn't need to be there!

What can you do with that thought now that you have caught it?

# Chapter 13
# What to do with Worries

By doing the activities in this section you will be helping your child to:

- see that there are lots of different ways of handling worries
- identify useful worry-solving/problem-solving skills.

## 1. A worry shared (p.119)

Ask your child to draw something that worries her.

*Talk about:*

- Writing a worry down or telling someone else often helps to make it seem less troublesome.

- When you are worried, is it the whole of you that feels worried or just a part of you? How much of you believes that your worry will really happen?

- Who do you share your worries with? Can you think of someone who could be your 'worry buddy'?

## 2. The worry box (p.120)

Complete the activity sheet together.

Make a brightly coloured 'worry box' and invite your child to post any worries that he might have. Set aside a particular time, as often as you feel is necessary, to check the worry box together and to 'problem-solve' any worries that are there.

Remind your child that he doesn't need to think about the worries once he has written them down, because they will be dealt with during the designated worry-busting time. If your child is particularly anxious, you may find that you need a worry-busting time every day to begin with, but that this will gradually reduce. Don't be concerned if the same or similar worries are repeated. This problem-solving should be a joint effort.

Try not to 'rescue' the situation by giving your child advice about what to do. Really listen to her concerns and worries without any judgement as to their validity or not. Your child may have some suggestions about what she would like to happen with regard to these worries. Some of these may not be realistic, but you can acknowledge the wish behind them.

For example, your child is worried that there is a monster under her bed. She wants you to stay in the room with her until she goes to sleep. You could acknowledge her need to have a strong grown-up whom she trusts to keep her safe from 'scary' things. Then explore what else would help her to feel in control of scary thoughts. Make your own suggestions, too, but be prepared for your child to reject these if they don't feel quite right!

Encourage your child to think of lots of different solutions with you and to pick her own strategies from a selection. This can be far more effective than telling a child just one way of dealing with a worry.

Set limits on worries or times of worries. If your child asks you to check the worries outside the designated time, reassure her that she will have time to think about them later, but that there are other things to think about and to do before then.

Once the worry has been resolved, or your child feels that she is coping with it, then the piece of 'worry' paper can be torn up.

## 3. The HugMe tree (p.121)

Sometimes, if worries can't be dealt with immediately, they can be deposited or off-loaded somewhere. The HugMe tree is designed to be just such a place (but it needs a hug afterwards!). The HugMe tree can also be used for hanging up worries before your child goes to sleep.

### The HugMe tree

Close your eyes and settle yourself into a comfortable position. Take three full, relaxed breaths…

Allow your imagination to take you to a magic mountain. Imagine that you are standing in a field at the bottom of this mountain, ready to go on a walk… [wait a moment for your child to begin to get an image]. In front of you there is a gate. Walk slowly towards it… It's a very special gate. Can you see what it is made of?… Is there anything growing around it?… What does it feel like when you touch it?… When you are ready, imagine yourself going through this gate and standing on the other side.

Close the gate carefully behind you. You are standing on a path that leads up the mountain… You are going to look for the HugMe tree. It is near the gate somewhere. Have a look around at all the trees until you see the biggest one. This is the HugMe tree. It's so huge that it seems to go on for ever up into the sky… Stand right up against the tree and touch the bark… What does it feel like? You can hang up all your worries on its branches before you explore any more of the mountain. The HugMe tree is so big that it can take as many worries as you like, so long as you give it a hug afterwards! Imagine yourself leaving your worries here. What does that feel like?

Now let's take five steps.

One... What did that feel like?...

Two... What can you see?...

Three... What can you hear?...

Four... What can you smell?...

Five... What are you feeling now?...

Stand still for a moment and take a full breath... Breathe out with a long sigh. Feel yourself being as strong as the mountain itself... You're full of confidence and ready to go on... Imagine yourself exploring all around this part of the mountain. Keep noticing what your body feels like when you are worry-free. What can you feel? What can you see? [Allow your child a few moments to explore the mountain in their imagination.]

It's time to leave the mountain for today. Begin to walk back towards the HugMe tree... Now you are near the gate... Go through the gate and close it again behind you... Step into the field. Take a full breath and let it go with a big sigh...

Now start to think about your toes and your fingers. Give them a little wriggle... Keep your eyes closed and feel how your body is gradually back in the room where you started. Notice the feel of your clothes against your skin, and your body touching the chair... Still keep your eyes closed for a little while longer. Begin to listen to the sounds in the room and outside... Now wriggle your toes and fingers again, and when you're ready, have a big stretch and a yawn and open your eyes... And here you are back in the room!

## 4. The worry team (p.122)

Complete the activity sheet together.

*Talk about:*

- What could happen to your worries? 'What would you like your worries to do? Imagine this happening. What happens next? Then what happens?'

  For example, worries can disappear, grow bigger, shrink, or change into something else. We could make friends with them, throw them away, send them to the moon, or take them to 'obedience' classes!

- Encourage fantasy solutions as well as more practical ones. For example: they could be tied up in a bundle and sent to _____, who would read each one and discuss them with _____. Laws would be passed to make

_____ illegal. Everyone who had ever worried about _____ would receive _____. All the worries would then be _____.

- Is there such a thing as a 'useful' worry? What would life be like if we never had any worries?

## 5. A problem halved

Lots of children are reluctant or even afraid to ask for help when they need it. They may feel that this is further evidence that they are failing and may therefore use other strategies, such as watching other children and following their lead, or perhaps waiting passively until someone *offers* help. Feeling that it is OK to ask someone to repeat an instruction, or that it is OK to say 'I don't understand', is a big step for many children. Talking about this in a very 'matter-of-fact' way can help them to feel that it is a natural part of the learning process, rather than a failure.

Help your child to think about what to do for some common problems – for example, you forget to take your lunch to school; your pet hamster gets out of its cage; you accidentally break something in school; someone borrows your pencils and keeps forgetting to give them back; you sometimes don't understand what your teacher has asked you to do.

*Talk about:*

Some worries are about problems that can be solved. Some worries are about things that can't be solved – but these worries *can* be tamed! It's good to know which sort of worry you are thinking about.

Possible strategies might include:

- Ask someone to explain it to me.
- Talk to my 'worry buddy' about it.
- Break the instruction down into smaller bits and do one bit at a time.
- Ask for a repetition of the instruction/question.

Encourage recognition of previous experiences of problem-solving. It is helpful if children can realise that every time they solve a problem, they are creating new possibilities for themselves.

## 6. The magical Book of Wisdom (p.123)

### The Book of Wisdom

Let your eyes gently close and feel your body relaxing…
Imagine yourself at the foot of the magic mountain by the HugMe tree. Do you want to give the tree a hug today?

Maybe you didn't notice at first, but tucked away in the roots of the HugMe tree there is a very special, magical book. Can you tell me when you have found it?…

What does it look like?

This book contains answers to so many questions that it's thought to be one of the most precious books in the whole world. Carefully open the cover and look at the first page. Do you see that it says 'Worries' in silver letters? Do you have a worry at the moment that you'd like to ask the book about? Have a think and see if there's anything you might like to know while you're here.

**[If there is a worry]** Now, if you tell the book your worry it will be able to give you a little bit of help. You might have to wait for some time while it finds the right piece of wisdom to tell you, but be patient and it will come. This book is so special that it can tell you things in lots of different ways. It might show you a picture or some writing, or it might whisper back to you. So now you just have to keep looking at the book and wait. Will you tell me when you've got your answer?… Now, because it's very special to be able to talk to this book, it would be nice to thank it for its wisdom and close it very gently.

**[If there is no worry]** OK, no worries today. Maybe you might want to come back another time to have a look. Close the book very gently.

It's time to leave now. You thank the HugMe tree for letting you look in the book. You start to walk back towards the gate… Go through the gate and close it again behind you… And now you're back in the field. Take a full breath and let it go with a big sigh.

As you stand in the field, take three more full breaths… Now start to think about your toes and your fingers. Give them a little wriggle… Keep your eyes closed and feel how your body is gradually back in the room where you started. Notice the feel of your clothes against your skin, and your body touching the chair… Still keep your eyes closed for a little while longer. Begin to listen to the sounds in the room and outside… Now wriggle your toes and fingers again, and when you're ready have a big stretch and a yawn and open your eyes… And here you are, back in the room!

I'm sure that most of us have had the experience of coming up with a solution to a difficult problem when we were least expecting it. We think about it for hours and come to no conclusions; so we give up and go for a walk, and suddenly the answer seems crystal clear! Or perhaps you have tried to think of a name or a song title but couldn't remember it – then suddenly, there it is – just as you are falling asleep that night. Once again, naming the problem or defining the question can help to take some of the worry out of it. Inevitably the child's innate wisdom will help to sort it, even if that wisdom tells him to ask someone for help.

### 7. Taming troublesome tigers (p124)

Take turns to think up ideas for taming worries that are getting out of control.

*Talk about:*

- Even when worries are useful, they need to be kept in proportion, or 'tamed'. We don't want them to leap out at us unexpectedly or follow us around constantly, growling at us and making us fearful. We need to respect the wisdom of these worries – but also show them who is boss!

### 8. Story treasures (4)

Read a story about worries, or a story about a perfect day.

Make up your own stories about worries, for example, 'The Day the Worries Took Over the School!'

My books about worries became well-worn very quickly! I like the classic Dr Seuss book *I Had Trouble in Getting to Solla Sollew* (age 6+) – a 'fable' about facing up to your troubles. Also popular amongst the children (and, I have to say, amongst many of my colleagues!) is *The Huge Bag of Worries* by Virginia Ironside, suitable for all age groups. Wonderfully illustrated by Frank Rodgers, this is the story of a young girl whose bag of worries gets bigger and bigger, and no one seems to be able to help until the old lady from next door suggests something radical – open it up and show the worries some daylight!

I have also used *I'm Worried* by Brian Moses (age 4+), one of the 'Your Feelings' series. This contains notes for parents and teachers, with lots of suggestions for group activities and discussions.

### 9. Make a plan

Outline different situations and talk about what children might specifically do, using ideas from all the activity sheets completed. Making a plan will help your child to feel more in control of her worries. Encourage her to think of at least three things that she can do for each situation. For example:

- When X happens, I will _____, or _____, or _____
- When I notice myself getting uptight/feeling cross, I will _____
- When I feel happy, I will _____

## 10. Drawing things together (p.125)

Draw pictures together of times when you and your child are 'worry free'.

## 11. Unwind

Do a relaxation session and tape it, so that your child can use this whenever she wants to (thus taking control over her own relaxation on a regular basis). See previous ideas for coping with stress in Chapters 10 and 11.

## A worry shared

**Draw a picture of something
you are worried about**

## The worry box

Imagine that you could put your worries into a worry box and close the lid.

What do you think should happen to them then? Where would they go? Would anyone look at them? If so, who would it be? What would they do with them?

Draw or write about what happens.

## The HugMe tree

Imagine that there is a tree called the HugMe tree. It is so big and has so many branches that it can take all your worries for you.

Draw or write about any worries you might have, and hang them on the branches. You can use the HugMe tree at night to hang up your worries before you go to sleep. Just picture it in your mind.

Imagine yourself giving the HugMe tree a great big hug!

## The worry team

Imagine that you are part of a worry team.

This is a group of exceptionally clever people who spend their time inventing ways of getting rid of worries.

They thought of the HugMe tree and the worry box. Make a list of other things that you could do with worries. How inventive can you be?

## Let's imagine...the BOOK OF WISDOM

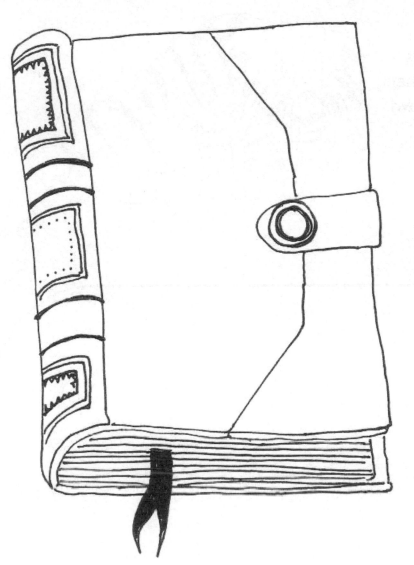

Imagine that you have a special book. A book that knows the answer to lots of different questions. It is especially good at solving worry problems.

When you talk to this book, it always listens, and sooner or later it always comes up with an answer.

Sometimes, the answer doesn't come straight away.

Sometimes you have to wait a few days, and then – just when you least expect it – you'll know what to do!

## Taming troublesome tigers

Think of all the things that you could do when a worry starts to growl at you!

## Drawing things together

**Draw a picture of you
when you are worry-free**

*Part Six*

# Moving On

## Chapter 14

# Setting Goals and Celebrating

By doing the activities in this section you will be helping your child to:

- explore the idea of setting regular goals
- develop strategies for monitoring his own progress
- celebrate his achievements in coping with change, stress or anxiety.

### 1. Spaceship to the stars (p.132)

This activity is adapted from an original exercise by Dina Glouberman (Glouberman 2003, p.186). Projecting yourself into the future to imagine how things will turn out is a powerful aid to making changes. Such imagery requires the suspending of judgement and reality in order to act 'as if' you had already achieved your desired outcome.

This imagework exercise will be most effective if your child has a particular goal in mind before starting.

#### Just the right star

Find a comfortable position…and gently let your eyes close. Take three full breaths, breathing in right down into the bottom of your lungs and breathing out slowly and calmly.

Let's imagine that you can travel into the future in your own special spaceship. Imagine what that spaceship looks like… What colour is it?… What shape?

Notice what it sounds like. Can you see the spaceship door?…

If you go inside you will see a really comfortable chair to sit in, with some controls on a board in front of it and a large window that goes at least halfway around the ship.

Imagine yourself sitting at the controls. There are lots of them. There's a button that has a sign under it saying 'To the stars' and one that says 'Back home'.

When you're ready to go, all you have to do is press the button for the stars and the spaceship will gently take off and head up into the sky. You will be totally in control. Ready?…

You're climbing high up into the sky now… You are travelling through the clouds. The sky around you is becoming a deeper and deeper blue, and you can see the stars shining ahead of you. You're going high into the place where everything and anything is possible…

Somewhere up here is your own special star… Search around for a little while until you can see it clearly in front of you… Have you found it?… Notice all the little details about this very special star as the spaceship hovers near it and circles around it… If there is something you have to get done, or a goal you want to set for yourself, then this star will be able to show you what things will be like for you once you've achieved it. If you've thought of something, you can try it out now – or, if not, you can come back again another time. Tell me if there is something you'd like to be able to do…

Now, imagine that there is a beam of light shining out from the star into the sky. It can project pictures onto the sky as though you were at the cinema. As you watch, you can see a big screen forming in the sky ahead of you. Onto this screen walks a person… It's you! This is you after you've achieved your goal. **[If you know what your child's goal is, it would be helpful to name it at this point. For example, 'You've finished your maths test', 'You've learnt how to swim', 'You can ride your new bike', 'You've finished making that model and it's right there beside you'.]**

What do you look like on the screen?… What is the 'future you' doing now?… What did you do to make this happen?… What did you need to have or to know so that you could achieve your goal?… How is 'you' on the screen different from you sitting in the spaceship?… If the future you could whisper something special to you in the spaceship, what would they whisper?…

The future you says goodbye and is walking away now. As you watch, the beam of light from the star starts to get fainter and the screen starts to fade, until eventually it has disappeared altogether… How are you feeling now?

If you like, you've got plenty of time just to play up here in the stars. You can make your spaceship go wherever you want. See what you can find up here! **[Let your child explore in silence for a few minutes.]**

Time now to leave the stars. Take one last look around… Press the button that says 'Back home', and away goes the spaceship, through the deep blue sky…through the floating clouds…slowly and gently back down to earth…

Now you have landed safely. As you get out of the spaceship, notice if you feel any different now to how you felt when you first set off…

Now you're walking away from the spaceship. Feel yourself coming back to the room… Notice the feel of your body… Listen to the sounds around you… Keep your eyes closed for a little while longer while you have a little stretch…

When you are ready, open your eyes and look around you... Stamp your feet on the floor a bit to bring you properly back down to earth!

## 2. Future me (p.133)

Invite your child to write a letter to himself from the future, telling himself how he achieved his goals.

## 3. My treasure chest (p.134)

Talk about the different treasures that your child chooses. Make regular times when he can 'find' something in his treasure chest.

## 4. I can change the way I feel

Help your child to identify a 'toolkit' of things that she is going to do to keep up her confidence (or whatever her main goal is). She can then use this list to check off each achievement. The aim is also to help children to see that the skills and qualities they already have from other areas of life (such as perseverance and practice) can be put to good use when they are setting their goals. A possible list might be:

- I will reward myself when I have done well.
- I will take care of myself by doing something relaxing every day.
- I will answer at least one question in class every day.
- I will learn to swim.
- I will learn one new word every day.
- I will tell my teacher if I don't understand something.
- I will talk to my mum about my worries.
- I will make one new friend this term.

## 5. Emblems of success

Draw the shape of a shield on a large piece of paper. Divide the shield into four sections and draw different symbols or pictures in each section to show successful strategies that your child uses in order to achieve his goals. Possible strategies might be:

- talking with a friend
- asking for help to solve a difficulty
- listening to some relaxing music
- respecting and valuing myself
- finding a quiet space to 'chill out'.

## Spaceship to the stars

Draw or write about your special star.

## Future me

Take some time to write a special letter to yourself from the future, telling yourself how to work on your goal.

_____

_____

_____

_____

_____

_____

_____

_____

_____

_____

_____

_____

## My treasure chest

Let's imagine that you have a treasure chest that is full of all the wonderful things about being you.

Can you imagine the chest? What is it made of? How big is it?

Imagine that every bit of treasure somehow shows us something special about you. Each piece of treasure has a label on it to show us what it is.

It would be a shame to keep all that treasure shut away in the chest all the time, don't you think?

Imagine that every day you go to your treasure chest and take a few things out to put on show so that we can all admire it.

What treasure will you choose today?

From my treasure chest today I chose _____

_____

_____

_____

# References

Glouberman, D. (2003) *Life Choices, Life Changes.* London: Hodder and Stoughton.

# Children's Books

*And to Think that I Saw It on Mulberry Street* by Dr Seuss (HarperCollins, 1992)

*Bill's New Frock* by Anne Fine (Mammoth Books, 1999)

*Fergus the Forgetful* by Margaret Ryan and Wendy Smith (Collins, 1995)

*I had Trouble in Getting to Solla Sollew* by Dr Seuss (HarperCollins Children's Books, 1998)

*I'm Scared* by Bel Money (Mammoth Books, 1998)

*I'm Worried* by Brian Moses (Wayland Publishers Ltd, 1997)

*Nothing* by Mick Inkpen (Hodder Children's Books,1996)

*Only a Show* by Anne Fine (Puffin Books, 1998)

*Scaredy Cat* by Anne Fine (Mammoth Books, 1998)

*Something Else* by Kathryn Cave and Chris Riddell (Picture Puffins, 1995)

*The Afterdark Princess* by Annie Dalton (Mammoth, 2001)

*The Dream Snatcher* by Annie Dalton (Mammoth, 2001)

*The Huge Bag of Worries* by Virginia Ironside (Macdonald Young Books, 1998)

*The Midnight Museum* by Annie Dalton (Mammoth, 2001)

# Index

activities
  celebrations 129–34
  coping with worries 112–25
  dealing with stress 96–103
  feelings 58–65
  goal setting 129–34
  imagework 50–7
  making a change 84–6
  preparing for change 78–83
  recognising worries 107–11
  self-awareness 41–9
  understanding stress 89–95
  thinking about change 69–77
*Afterdark Princess, The* (Dalton) 54
amygdala 22
*And to Think That I Saw It on*
  *Mulberry Street* (Dr Seuss) 54
anxiety activities
  coping with worries 112–25
  recognising worries 107–11
attachment
  as stress factor 24

Bandler, R. 34
*Bill's New Frock* (Fine) 44
brain
  and amygdala 22
  and emotional regulation
    22–3
  and pre-frontal cortex 22–3
breath control
  and emotional regulation 28

Cave, K. 44
celebration activities 129–34

change activities
  making a change 84–6
  preparation for change
    78–83
  thinking about change 69–76
*Chasing Ideas* (Durham) 19
communication disorders
  as stress factor 24

Dalton, A. 54
*Dream Snatcher, The* (Dalton) 54
Durham, C. 19

Einstein, A. 36
Eliot, L. 24
emotional regulation
  and the brain 22–3
  and breath control 28
  and communication disorders
    24
  and imagery usage 26–7,
    28–9
  and massage 28
  and physical activity 27–8
  relaxation techniques 27
  and touch 28
emotions
  expression of 16–17
  valuing 16–17 *see also*
    feelings activities

feelings *see* emotions
feelings activities 58–65
*Fergus the Forgetful* (Ryan and
  Smith) 74

Fine, A. 44, 73

Gerhardt, S. 23
Glouberman, D. 32, 129
goal setting activities 129–34
Grinder, J. 34

Hillman, J. 32
*Huge Bag of Worries, The*
  (Ironside) 117

*I Had Trouble in Getting to Solla*
  *Sollew* (Dr Seuss) 117
*I'm Scared* (Mooney) 74
*I'm Worried* (Moses) 117
images
  creation of 30–1
  and emotional regulation
    26–7, 28–9
  and imagework 31–3
  and migraines 29
  uniqueness of 32–3
imagework
  activities for 50–7
  and coping with change
    34–6
  creation of 32
  description of 31–2
  exercises 33
  and goal setting 33–4
  guidelines for 36–7
'Imaginal Practice' (Hillman) 32
imagination *see* images
Inkpen, M. 44
Ironside, V. 117

Jung, C. 32

massage
    and emotional regulation 28
*Midnight Museum, The* (Dalton)
    54
Mooney, B. 74
Moses, B. 117

neuroscience
    developments in 21–2
*Nothing* (Inkpen) 44
Nunn, K. 22

Olness, K. 29
*Only a Show* (Fine) 73

physical activity
    and emotional regulation
        27–8
praise
    problems with 18
    strategies for 18–19
    value of 17
pre-frontal cortex 22–3

relaxation techniques
    and emotional regulation 27
Riddell, C. 44
Rogers, C. 15
Ryan, M. 74

*Scaredy Cat* (Fine) 73
self-awareness activities 41–9
Seuss, Dr 54, 117
Smith, W. 74
*Something Else* (Cave and Riddell)
    44
stress
    activities to deal with
        96–103
    activities to understand
        89–95
    and attachment 24
    common stress factors 24

and communication disorders
    24
description of 23
effects of 25–6
stress response 25
symptoms of 26
Sunderland, M. 26, 28

Tart, C. 27
touch
    and emotional regulation 28

worries activities
    coping with worries 112–25
    recognising worries 107–11

# Activities Index

NB (number in italics) *indicates activities and information sheets for parents*

A problem halved 115
A worry shared 112, *119*
Acknowledge and celebrate 80
Acting up 60
A focus relaxation 99
All change 69

Being in balance 59
Big and small 71
Build a 'refuelling station' 96

Catching thoughts 108, 111
Check in regularly 85
Confidence for change (1) 71
Confidence for change (2) 72

Different ways of thinking 90
Drawing things together 118 *125*

Emblems of success 131
Emotion masks 60
Encourage friendships 85
Everyone is different 42
Experiments 71
Explore 80

Feeling good about being me 53, *57*
Feelings 90, *95*

Feeling tense and feeling relaxed 91
Fidget flop 98
Figure it out 62
Future me 131, *133*

Get creative 85
Get messy 97
Giggle switch 98
Good news and bad news 108

Help the wizard and Grimes to solve the riddle 72, *75*
How many feelings? 58, *63*
How I feel 58, *64*
How to make my perfect day 101, *103*
Humour 97

I am me 42, *46*
I can change the way I feel 131
If feelings were colours 59, *65*
If I were an animal 65
I packed my suitcase 78
Imagine making a change 79
Involvement 78
Is this how you see me? 42

Junk thoughts 107, 110
Just because 108
Just hanging loose! 100

Keep things in proportion 85

Let's imagine 72, *76*

Make a plan 117
Massage197
Meet the brain 89, *93*
Mixing it up 107
Model the desired response 86
Musical drawing 98
My display cabinet 43, *48*
My record of achievements 44
My treasure chest 131, *134*

Parent questions 11
Pass a smile 97
Prepare to dive! 78, *81*

Quick draw 71

Reassure 80
Relaxed breathing 96
Research 79

Seek support 86
Self-portraits 41, *45*
Show me how you feel 58
Skills for change 70
Snowmen 92
Some stress can be good for you 90, *94*
Something in common? 43, *47*
Spaceship to the stars 129, *132*
Steps along the way 79, *83*

Story treasures (1) 44
Story treasures (2) 53
Story treasures (3) 73
Story treasures (4) 117
Stressed out! 89

Taking care of myself every day
    101, *102*
Talking cats 51, *56*
Taming troublesome tigers 117,
    *124*
Tell me my story 53
The 6 'R's 84
The worry box 112, *120*
The HugMe tree 113, *121*
The worry team 114, *122*
The magical Book of Wisdom
    115, *123*
Things I would like to achieve
    44, *49*
Think of a chocolate cake 50

Unwind 118

'Waves on the sea' parachute
    game 61
What are images? 50, *55*
What is change? 70
What shall we do with them? 61
When I want to calm myself 99
Word play 69
Worry town 109